W9-ASR-246

PRAYING GRACE

55 Meditations
and Declarations
on the Finished
Work of Christ

DAVID A. HOLLAND

BroadStreet
PUBLISHING

BroadStreet Publishing Group, LLC.
Savage, Minnesota, USA
Broadstreetpublishing.com

Praying Grace: *55 Meditations and Declarations on the Finished Work of Christ*

Copyright ©2020 Inprov, Ltd.

978-1-4245-6116-2 (softcover)
978-1-4245-6118-6 (faux leather)
978-1-4245-6117-9 (ebook)

All rights reserved. Except as permitted under the U.S. Copyright Act of 1976, no part of this publication may be reproduced, distributed, or transmitted in any form or by any means, or stored in a database or retrieval system, without the prior written permission of the publisher.

Scripture quotations marked (AMP) are taken from the Amplified® Bible, Copyright © 2015 by The Lockman Foundation. Used by permission. www.lockman.org. Scriptures are taken from the English Standard Version® (ESV®), Copyright © 2001 by Crossway, a publishing ministry of Good News Publishers. All rights reserved. Scripture quotations marked (CJB) are taken from the Common Jewish Bible. Copyright © 1998 by David H. Stern. All rights reserved. Scripture quotations marked (HCSB) are taken from the Holman Christian Standard Bible®, Copyright © 1999, 2000, 2002, 2003, 2009 by Holman Bible Publishers. Used by permission. Holman Christian Standard Bible®, Holman CSB®, and HCSB® are federally registered trademarks of Holman Bible Publishers. Scripture quotations marked (MEV) are taken from the Modern English Version. Copyright © 2014 by Military Bible Association. Used by permission. All rights reserved. Scripture quotations marked (MSG) are taken from *THE MESSAGE*, Copyright © 1993, 1994, 1995, 1996, 2000, 2001, 2002 by Eugene H. Peterson. Used by permission of NavPress. All rights reserved. Represented by Tyndale House Publishers, Inc. Scripture quotations marked (NASB) are taken from the New American Standard Bible®, Copyright ©1960, 1962, 1963, 1968, 1971, 1972, 1973, 1975, 1977, 1995 by The Lockman Foundation, La Habra, CA. All rights reserved. Used by Permission. www.lockman.org. Scripture quotations marked (NIV) are taken from the Holy Bible, New International Version®, NIV®. Copyright © 1973, 1978, 1984, 2011 by Biblica, Inc.™ Used by permission of Zondervan. All rights reserved worldwide. www.zondervan.com The "NIV" and "New International Version" are trademarks registered in the United States Patent and Trademark Office by Biblica, Inc.™ Scripture quotations marked (NKJV) are taken from the New King James Version®. Copyright © 1982 by Thomas Nelson. Used by permission. All rights reserved. Scripture quotations marked (NLT) are taken from the Holy Bible, New Living Translation, Copyright ©1996, 2004, 2015 by Tyndale House Foundation. Used by permission of Tyndale House Publishers, Inc., Carol Stream, Illinois 60188. All rights reserved. Tree of Life (TLV) Translation of the Bible. Copyright © 2015 by The Messianic Jewish Family Bible Society. Scripture quotations marked (TPT) are from The Passion Translation®. Copyright © 2017, 2018 by Passion & Fire Ministries, Inc. Used by permission. All rights reserved. ThePassionTranslation.com. Scripture quotations marked (VOICE) are taken from The Voice™. Copyright © 2012 by Ecclesia Bible Society. Used by permission. All rights reserved.

Design by Chris Garborg | garborgdesign.com

Editorial services by Michelle Winger | literallyprecise.com

Printed in the United States of America.
20 21 22 23 24 25 26   7 6 5 4 3 2 1

CONTENTS

FOREWORD

Laurie and I have been profoundly impacted by the liberating message of grace we have received in recent years. We've been amazed at the results as we've learned to pray *from* victory instead of praying *for* victory.

It's no exaggeration to say that a fuller understanding of the wonders of God's grace has transformed our lives and enriched our walk with God in countless ways. But in no area has that transformation been greater than in the area of our prayer lives.

Understanding that God's throne truly is a throne of grace; grasping the full scope of Jesus's finished work on the cross; and getting a deeper revelation of God's goodness and faithfulness has changed us. Each of these discoveries have combined to make our praying more exciting and more effective. Far more effective!

That's why we welcome this devotional by David A. Holland. We're thrilled to be able to direct friends to a resource that will help them renew their minds to the realities of grace, and model grace-based praying for them. This devotional takes you by the hand and, in 55 days, teaches you how to pray *from* a clear understanding of the victory Jesus has already won for you.

In the Bible, the number "5" symbolizes grace. That makes "55" an excellent number for the meditations and prayers on the pages that follow. We encourage you to spend some time with each of these for the next 55 days. We're confident you'll discover what we have learned. Namely, that life becomes much more exciting and fulfilling when you learn to pray grace-based prayers.

Matt & Laurie Crouch

INTRODUCTION

"I wish I could point people to a resource that taught believers how to pray *from* victory rather than *for* victory."

That off-hand comment by TBN President Matt Crouch during a phone call provided the inspiration for the unique devotional you hold in your hands. When I heard the phrase "praying from victory," I immediately recognized the powerful paradigm to which Matt was referring.

He was talking about an utterly biblical, but poorly understood, way of approaching prayer that has profoundly impacted my own prayer life. Which is why I quickly raised my hand and said I would love to have the privilege of fulfilling that wish.

Creating this devotional was a labor of love and passion. The revolutionary truths that unfold on these pages are precious to me. They've not only transformed my life and relationship with my heavenly Father, they've enabled me to pray with more power and efficacy than I dreamed possible. Indeed, I have told the members of The Cup & Table Co.—the wonderful community of believers it is my privilege to pastor and teach—that this book contains the things that I most want the people I love to understand and embrace.

I want you to understand and embrace these liberating truths, too. I know that if you will, you'll never pray the same way again. Each devotional concludes with a declarative prayer. In other words, a prayer that puts you in the position of partnering with God by giving voice to His will for you and for those around you.

Get ready to discover the power and joys of *Praying Grace*.

David A. Holland

Escape the "Try Harder" Trap

There remains, then, a Sabbath-rest for the people of God; for anyone who enters God's rest also rests from their works, just as God did from his.

HEBREWS 4:9–10 NIV

It has been said that the last 2,000 years of teaching and preaching on how to successfully live the Christian life and please God could actually be encapsulated in a simple two-word exhortation:

Try harder.

Do you keep stumbling over the same sin or habit? *Try harder.* Are you struggling to love unlovely and obnoxious people? *Try harder.* Failing time and again to rise an hour early for prayer and Bible reading? *Try harder.* Not giving enough? Serving enough? Witnessing enough? Attending church services enough? *Try harder.*

You know the prescription. Bear down. Double up. Lather, rinse, repeat—in an endless, frustrating, shame-soaked cycle of defeat and failure that robs you of your confidence before God and keeps you feeling like the only Christian in the world who isn't properly doing all the things.

None of that sounds very restful, does it? Yet, rest is precisely what we are called to in Jesus; particularly, rest from striving and straining to earn God's approval.

The fact is, God sent Jesus so we could become restful human *beings*, not busy human *doings*. God paid an enormous price and lavished His grace upon us to restore us—not to good behavior—but to Himself, to reconnect us to the Source of life and love.

When you live and rest in that connection, all those other good and noble things overflow out of your life organically and effortlessly. Witnessing: the peace, joy, and confidence that shines from you when you rest in Him becomes an irresistible beacon to the lost and hurting. Love: when you are secure in God's love and acceptance, you become unoffendable, and naturally capable of more patience and grace than you thought possible.

We have all tried the "try harder" approach. It doesn't work. Grace does.

PRAYER OF DECLARATION

Heavenly Father, I cease from my futile labors. I no longer strive to earn what I cannot possibly earn, to merit what I will never deserve. Instead, I rejoice and rest in my connection to You through Your Son. He is the vine, and I am a connected branch.

I declare today that in Jesus, Your love, Your power, Your goodness, and Your empowering grace all flow through me—producing fruit naturally, and shaping my desires and appetites.

Good and noble things overflow out of my life organically and effortlessly. Peace, joy, and confidence shine from me, making me an irresistible beacon to the lost and hurting. Because I am absolutely secure in Your love and acceptance, I am unoffendable, patient, and full of grace for others. For me, every day is a day of Sabbath rest.

"Tetelestai!"

So when Jesus had received the sour wine, He said, "It is finished!"
And bowing His head, He gave up His spirit.

JOHN 19:30 NKJV

The Savior's final words from the cross were a prayer of childlike faith: "Father, into your hands I entrust My spirit" (Luke 23:46 HCSB). Only moments earlier, the witnesses gathered around the dying Savior heard Him shout something else, a single word that was more of a Greek accounting term: "Tetelestai!"

Our English Bible translates that term in a way that drains it of the legal and financial connotations it clearly carried for hearers of Jesus' day. The best most can come up with is the plain-vanilla phrase, "It is finished."

Yet, *tetelestai* does not mean merely that a thing has concluded. It does not simply indicate that the curtain has come down and the show is over or "The End." No, to declare a thing *tetelestai* is to decree that *all* has been accomplished, everything formerly lacking has now been supplied. The wound has been healed. The obligation has been met. The debt has been completely satisfied!

Jesus' *Tetelestai!* declared an end to man's Tower-of-Babel religious striving to build a ladder back to heaven. God Himself had come down and done what no fallen man could do: satisfy mankind's staggering legal and spiritual obligation to divine justice.

In an 1861 sermon, Charles Spurgeon explained what Jesus meant when He cried from the cross, "It is finished!"

> The Savior meant that the satisfaction which He rendered to the justice of God was finished. The debt was now, to the last farthing, all discharged. The atonement and propitiation were made once for all, and forever, by the one offering made in Jesus's body on the tree (*Metropolitan Tabernacle Pulpit Volume 7*, Sermon 47, December 1, 1861).

Powerful, grace-based praying begins with an understanding of Jesus' cry of *tetelestai*. To pray prayers of grace starts with the humbling, liberating realization that Christ has done all the work for our atonement. All that remains is to receive it.

TO DECLARE A THING

TETELESTAI IS TO DECREE

THAT *ALL* HAS BEEN

ACCOMPLISHED.

Prayer of Declaration

Father, I thank You for sending Jesus to pay my debt in full. Through His sacrifice, the demands of holy justice woven into the fabric of the universe at the moment of creation have been fully satisfied. I rejoice in the glorious truth that I can come to You with no sense of obligation, indebtedness, or shame.

Lord Jesus, thank You for Your willingness to come. I will not insult Your grace by seeking to add a single thing to a work You declared complete with your shout of "Tetelestai!" nor will I try to pay against a debt You have declared, "Paid in full." I will humble myself and gratefully receive everything You died to provide for me; everything Your Word declares is mine.

I have everything I need pertaining to life and godliness, down to the smallest detail. Your will is being done in my life here on earth just as it is in heaven!

Praying from Rest

For the one who has entered His rest has himself also rested from his works,
as God did from His. Therefore let us be diligent to enter that rest,
so that no one will fall, through following the same example of disobedience.
HEBREWS 4:10–11 NASB

Adam and Eve's labor to create fig leaf garments to cover their shame represents mankind's very first religious work. Cain's rejected offering was the second (and that rejection led to the first murderous rage.)

From the Tower of Babel, to the meticulous rules and regulations of the Pharisees, to all the other world religions, right up to our modern day—fallen man's impulse has been to work or earn our way back into the Garden of Eden.

The coming of the Son of God to earth revealed that the Father had a very different plan for restoring us to His fellowship and blessings. One which would require nothing from us except the humility to recognize that we had nothing to contribute to our redemption, that our best attempts at righteousness were disgusting, smelly rags, and that all we could do is receive, enjoy, and share His blessings with others.

The writer of Hebrews compared this to God resting on day seven after six days of creation work. And, those who refuse to rest are compared to those Israelites who refused, through fear, to enter the Promised Land. We are exhorted to be extra sure—to "be diligent"—that we, too, have rested from our futile work.

Such diligence is necessary because it's so easy to slip back into works mode. We're surrounded by well-meaning people who try to make us afraid that we're not doing enough to earn or qualify for God's favor. Don't do it. Remain at rest. Pray from that position of rest.

PRAYER OF DECLARATION

Father, I recognize and accept that I have nothing to contribute to my redemption. Forgive me for ever trying to "sew fig leaves" to cover my shame or build my own tower back to You. I repent of trying to work or earn my way back into the "garden" of Your presence and to the sweetness of Your fellowship.

Today, I cease from my futile efforts to merit or qualify for Your acceptance and favor. I recognize that I have nothing to contribute to my own redemption. Instead, I choose rest. I rest wholly and completely in the finished work of Jesus. I celebrate it. I accept and receive restoration to the full fellowship of Your presence and a good life in the land of promise.

I will diligently remain at rest. I'll not slip back into works mode. I choose not to listen to the well-meaning voices of religion that would try to make me afraid that I'm not doing enough to earn or qualify for Your favor.

Father, from this position of rest, I humbly and gratefully receive and enjoy Your blessings and share them with others.

The Law, "Fulfilled"

*"Do not think that I have come to abolish the Law or the Prophets;
I have not come to abolish them but to fulfill them."*

MATTHEW 5:17 NIV

As we've seen, one of Jesus' final declarations from the cross was the phase, "It is finished!" He actually used the Greek word *tetelestai*. It was a Greek word commonly used in Jesus' time to signify that an obligation had been fully met, or that a debt had been paid completely.

The tense of the verb Jesus used (perfect passive indicative) means that an action has been completed, but that the results of that action will continue with full effect going forward. In other words, what Jesus accomplished on the cross was total and complete satisfaction of a debt, and it would continue to be paid in full for all time.

The Savior's use of this word clears up enormous confusion about another saying regarding the Law and the Prophets. Many well-meaning believers have taken Jesus' statement that He did not come to abolish the Law to mean that He was leaving the Old Covenant regulations in place.

Yet, His true meaning comes sharply into focus when you realize that the Old Covenant viewed the Law and its requirements as an *obligation* to be paid to God. And that failing to meet that obligation—failing to keep the Law—resulted in a *debt* to God. Paul had this sense of debt or obligation in mind when he wrote that Jesus "canceled out the certificate of debt consisting of decrees against us, which was hostile to us" (Colossians 2:14 NASB).

Simply abolishing the Law would have left the debt unpaid—the obligation unmet. But His glorious answer when He was asked if He came to *abolish* the Law was, "No. I came to *fulfill* it." In other words, "I have come to completely fulfill, once and for all, the obligation of the Law!"

We cannot satisfy our debt to the perfect, immutable law of God. And God, in His righteousness, cannot simply sweep that debt away with a wave of His hand. No, the obligation to the Law has to be satisfied.

Jesus did that for you and me. He fulfilled your obligation to the Law, and, as a result, you are debt free!

WHAT JESUS ACCOMPLISHED

ON THE CROSS WAS TOTAL AND

COMPLETE SATISFACTION OF A DEBT.

Prayer of Declaration

Father, I come to You confidently and without any sense of shame relating to any unpaid debt to Your perfect Law. Yes, I know I'm flawed and make mistakes, but I stand before You in Jesus' tetelestai—His "paid in full." I will not minimize the enormity and generosity of that gift by striving in my puny way to fulfill an enormous obligation He has already completely met.

I declare that Jesus has canceled out my certificate of debt: my legal obligation that consisted of hostile decrees against me. Instead, I follow the law of love—walking in generosity, kindness, and compassion toward others.

The Myth of the "Yes" Button

For in Him all the promises of God are "Yes."
Therefore also through Him is the "Amen" by us, to the glory of God.

2 CORINTHIANS 1:20 TLV

Ask a thousand believers if Christians should pray, and you'll get a thousand immediate "Yes!" answers. Ask the same group if they personally should pray more than they currently do, and again the response will be affirmative and unanimously, "Yes!" So, why don't we?

Few will admit the truth. Most don't pray (or pray more often) because they've tried it and found it a frustrating, bewildering exercise. Much of that frustration can be traced to a false assumption that can be described as the myth of the "Yes" button. Although they may not visualize it exactly in this way, most Christians sort of see God's throne having a big "Yes" button on one arm, which God sometimes pushes, thereby granting their wish.

If we have this paradigm in mind, we approach God with a request—perhaps for healing, rescue, or provision—and desperately hope He'll push the "Yes" button.

This invariably turns our prayer lives into a desperate, flailing, guessing game in which we randomly try different kinds of prayers and approaches to God in a frantic quest to find the one He's looking for, the one that will finally move His hand over to that button. We try the prayer of agreement, the prayer of petition, the Word-based prayer, prayer with fasting, prayer with repentance, and prayer with both fasting and repentance.

Because of this false premise, many eventually despair of ever finding the key to seeing an earthly manifestation of what the Bible clearly reveals to be God's will.

As the apostle Paul wrote in 2 Corinthians, seeing God's promises realized in our lives is a two-sided equation. It requires God's "Yes" (His expressed will) and our "Amen" (belief or faith that He will do it). And we already have God's "Yes!" in Jesus.

At the risk of taking the metaphor too far, Jesus pressed the "Yes" button when He took His seat on the throne at God's right hand. If you are in Christ and He is in you, all of God's promises belong to you. God is continually giving His "Yes" concerning those promises to you; He has already signed off on them because of your standing in Christ.

We simply need to add our confident, restful, assured, "Amen."

SEEING GOD'S PROMISES REALIZED IN OUR LIVES REQUIRES GOD'S YES AND OUR AMEN.

Prayer of Declaration

Father, thank You for Your everlasting "Yes" to Your promises through the work of Your Son and my Savior.

I qualify for everything Jesus's blood purchased for me. I no longer focus on myself, my flawed ways or failures and mistakes. My focus is on Jesus and His perfect fulfillment of everything needed for me to be in intimate relationship with You. I am not waiting for Your "Yes" concerning Your wonderful promises. In Jesus, healing, health, provision, peace, purpose, and power are already mine! Amen.

You, in Him—He, in You

"I am the vine, you are the branches; he who abides in Me and I in him,
he bears much fruit, for apart from Me you can do nothing."
JOHN 15:5 NASB

One of the magnificent, mysterious truths about the new birth is that it creates a state of being for the believer in which we are simultaneously *in* Jesus even as He is *in* us.

This truth is emphasized and reiterated over and over in the New Covenant, both in the words of Jesus and in the letters of Paul and John. In the first chapter of Ephesians alone, there are roughly a dozen occurrences of phrases like, "in Him," "in Christ," and "in Christ Jesus."

The full witness of the New Covenant is this: because we are in Jesus and He in us, we stand in His righteousness, His favor, and His authority. That is our legal position in the courts of heaven.

In fact, even though we remain here on earth, living out our daily lives, there is a very real sense in which we are also enthroned with Christ in heaven. This is the unambiguous message of Ephesians 2:6 (NIV): "And God raised us up with Christ and seated us with him in the heavenly realms **in Christ Jesus**" (emphasis added).

This means that you never come to God in prayer solely as yourself. For you, God's throne is a throne of grace you can approach boldly, confidently, and joyfully precisely because you come in Jesus and with Him *in* you (see Hebrews 4:16). And because you come in His righteousness, His favor, and His authority, you qualify for every great and precious promise in the Word:

> For no matter how many promises God has made, they are "Yes" in Christ. And so through him the "Amen" is spoken by us to the glory of God (2 Corinthians 1:20 NIV).

When your heart becomes convinced of this truth, the gratitude, joy, and adoration this produces in you fuels your worship and supercharges your faith to receive miracles—for others and for yourself.

BECAUSE WE ARE IN JESUS AND HE IN US, WE STAND IN HIS RIGHTEOUSNESS, HIS FAVOR, AND HIS AUTHORITY.

Prayer of Declaration

Father, I run boldly and confidently to You because I am in Jesus, and Jesus is in me. I know I am as received, welcomed, and favored as Your own beloved Son would be. I come into the courts of heaven clothed in Jesus' righteousness, His favor, and His authority.

In Christ, I stand fully qualified to receive every good and perfect gift from Your gracious hand.

But that's not all, dear Father. You've not only wrapped me in Your flawless Son, You've also seated me with Him upon His throne at Your right hand in heaven. That means I walk in this world as Christ's image bearer, wielding both His authority and His power as I move through my day.

Father, I worship You in awe and gratitude that such an extraordinary gift is mine.

The Conviction
of God's Fatherhood

So you have not received a spirit that makes you fearful slaves. Instead, you received God's Spirit when he adopted you as his own children. Now we call him, "Abba, Father." For his Spirit joins with our spirit to affirm that we are God's children. And since we are his children, we are his heirs.

ROMANS 8:15—17 NLT

How easy it is to fall into the trap of striving to *earn* your standing as a son or daughter of God; to constantly scratch and grope around for a fleeting feeling of acceptance or an elusive sense of worth based on your "good" behavior.

Like the embittered brother of the prodigal son, we can work, sacrifice, and struggle in a prideful quest to attain what is already fully ours. Or, like the prodigal himself, we can come to God with the mindset of a servant, feeling unworthy, unclean, and disqualified.

Neither son understood his true position or standing in the gracious heart of their father.

In a similar way, we desperately need a revelation that God is indeed our Father. That He has set His love upon us, drawn us with cords of love, and irrevocably adopted us as His own. Far too many believers live out their days with what has been called an "orphan spirit." This is simply a failure to recognize the truth about what God has done for you and in you. Most of all, that He adopted you as His own child.

The 19th century hymn writer F.W. Faber once said, "There is all the difference in the world between searching for evidences of my sonship and receiving the conviction of God's fatherhood. The one is an endless, profitless, soul-tormenting task; the other is light and liberty, the glorious liberty of the children of God."

Take your eyes off of yourself. Stop searching for evidence in your feelings or your actions that you are a child of God. Instead, look into the face of your Father. You'll see nothing but love and tenderness in those eyes. And the Spirit of God within you will spontaneously rise up in you and cry out, "Abba! My dear Father!"

God chose to be your Father. Believe it. Receive it. Pray like it.

WE DESPERATELY NEED A REVELATION THAT GOD IS INDEED OUR FATHER.

PRAYER OF DECLARATION

Abba Father, flood my soul with a revelation of Your Fatherhood to me. By Your Holy Spirit, fill me with an unshakeable conviction that I belong to You and that in Your house is where I truly belong.

Forgive me for ever striving to earn a place at Your table. May I not be like the prodigal son who comes with the mindset of a servant. Nor like the other brother who wrongly believed he was earning his reward through work or good behavior.

I declare that I rest confidently in the knowledge that I am forever, unchangeably, irrevocably Your child—not by virtue of what I have or haven't done, but because You have given me a spirit of adoption through which my inner spirit man joyfully cries out, "Papa!"

Faith Is a Force, Not a Work

And Jesus said to him, "Go; your faith has made you well."
Immediately he regained his sight and began following Him on the road.
MARK 10:52 NASB

Have you ever heard a description of faith that sounded a lot like performing well enough, long enough to earn God's approval? Or running for so long and so hard that you eventually cross some unseen, invisible finish line arbitrarily drawn by God?

Have you heard faith portrayed as some sort of spiritual muscle that you have to work strenuously and exhaustingly to build up? Have you heard anyone talk about accumulating enough faith to move God?

The fact is, genuine biblical faith is none of these things.

Don't misunderstand—faith is vitally important. Jesus constantly praised it, encouraged it, and was clearly disappointed when His disciples didn't have it. The word is used in the New Testament more than 250 times.

Faith is good and extraordinarily powerful. But faith isn't a work that qualifies you to receive an answer from God. Faith is the spiritual force that takes hold of the answer God has already joyfully provided. Another word for faith is simply *belief*.

When we *believe* God—believe in His utter goodness, kindness, and faithfulness; believe He is for us; believe His Word; believe that Jesus' sacrifice was all-sufficient, believe that our acceptance by God is based in Jesus' perfect performance and not our own—our faith reaches out and accesses what God has given.

In other words, faith isn't something you *do* to get God to move. It's the calm, confident assurance that He has already moved—that everything you could ever need has been abundantly supplied through Jesus' victory.

PRAYER OF DECLARATION

Father, I believe. But by a work of grace in my heart, increase even more my assurance, trust, and confidence in You. Like a well-fathered child, I know You are good and that You are for me. With my assurance in Your faithfulness, and in Jesus' amazing work of redemption, I receive what You provided through His sacrifice.

I declare that I believe You. I believe in Your utter goodness, Your unending kindness, and Your unwavering faithfulness. I believe You are for me. I believe what Your Word says about me.

I believe that Jesus' sacrifice was sufficient and all encompassing. So, today my faith confidently and expectantly reaches out and accesses all You have provided through the cross of Christ. I am filled with faith and confident expectancy.

Unspeakable Power

I also pray that you will understand the incredible greatness of God's power for us who believe him. This is the same mighty power that raised Christ from the dead and seated him in the place of honor at God's right hand in the heavenly realms.

EPHESIANS 1:19–20 NLT

Have you ever asked God for more spiritual power? If you did, did you truly expect to receive it? And if so, did you expect to receive a little or a lot?

Ponder for a moment the mind-blowing implications of today's Scripture.

Buried deep in the truth-rich recesses of Ephesians' extraordinary first chapter, those two verses speak of "the incredible greatness of God's power **for us**," and then they directly equate that power with the immense force that brought about Jesus' resurrection and enthroned Him at God's right hand.

Oh, what enormous power was required to loose the bonds of death that held Jesus in their grasp. If ever death wanted to hold onto a person, it was the One who truthfully declared, "I am the way, the truth, and the life" (see John 14:6).

Look closely at those verses one more time. Who is this astonishing power directed toward? It is "for us **who believe him.**" This power is not reserved for those who have earned it through good behavior and extra good works. It was not set aside as a special reward for an elite class of super-Christians.

No, simple belief is the only stated qualification here. As with almost every other blessing and benefit in God's remarkable kingdom of grace, childlike acceptance is the key to everything. "Do not be afraid; only believe," Jesus told the heartbroken Jairus who had just heard that his little daughter had died (Mark 5:36 NKJV).

That remains His request of us today. Unimaginable heavenly power is waiting to be deployed in you and for you; *only believe.*

PRAYER OF DECLARATION

Heavenly Father, just as Paul prayed for the Ephesians to have a fuller understanding of Your power, I ask this for myself today. Open the eyes of my understanding. Increase my faith. I choose, as an act of my will, to simply believe You today.

Oh Father, how incredibly great is Your power in me and for me!

I declare that the same mighty power that raised Christ from the dead and seated Him in the place of honor at Your right hand in the heavenly realms is now flowing through me to advance Your Kingdom and to accomplish everything that concerns me. I believe!

Pray Like a Commander,
Not a Beggar

*"Behold, I have given you authority to tread on serpents and scorpions,
and over all the power of the enemy, and nothing will injure you."*

Luke 10:19 NASB

Many believers were raised in well-meaning religious traditions that emphasized a certain type of humility. Genuine humility is indeed an important spiritual quality. It flows naturally from an awareness of how utterly powerless, helpless, and lost we are apart from Jesus. It comes from being mindful of the truth Jesus declared to His disciples: "Apart from Me you can do nothing" (John 15:5 NASB).

However, many Christians have been taught that even in Christ they remain worthless, miserable, lowly, sinful scum. This brand of false humility causes us to pray like beggars. We don't "come boldly to the throne of grace," as the writer of Hebrews exhorts (see Hebrews 4:16). Instead, we slink into God's presence on our bellies if we come to Him at all.

Christians with this shame-centered mindset tend to instinctively avoid engaging the Father who loves them and have difficultly receiving from Him when they do come to Him. They expect little and get precisely what they expect.

A New Covenant understanding of the believer's authority and position in Jesus will lead you to a very different mindset and a whole new level of praying!

Consider how Peter dealt with the lame man by the temple gate. Understanding the authority and power that was his in Jesus, Peter declared, "I have no silver and gold, but what I do have I give to you. In the name of Jesus Christ of Nazareth, rise up and walk!" (Acts 3:6 ESV) Notice those words: "what I do have I give."

Peter was no beggar, but as someone in rightful possession of blessings and power, he had authority to deploy and give away. What Peter gave came from the Lord. He clearly *had* it—both to possess and to give away.

Pray and declare today, not like a beggar, but like a commander to whom the King has delegated supernatural authority. With that authority, you can tread on all the power of the enemy and nothing will injure you.

CHRISTIANS WITH A SHAME-CENTERED MINDSET AVOID ENGAGING THE FATHER WHO LOVES THEM.

Prayer of Declaration

Father, I come boldly to Your throne of grace to receive help to move through this day in the authority You have gifted me in Jesus.

I declare that You have given me authority to tread on serpents and scorpions, and over all the power of the enemy. Nothing will injure me! As I encounter the works of the enemy, I will exercise that authority wisely and confidently to extend love and freedom to others, pushing back darkness wherever I go.

What I have freely received from You, I will freely give to others. I give encouragement. I give mercy. I share with others the life and power You've deposited in me.

The Radical Consistency
of Grace

*For it is by grace you have been saved, through faith—and this is not from
yourselves, it is the gift of God—not by works, so that no one can boast.*

EPHESIANS 2:8—9 NIV

God's grace doesn't play favorites. His abundant, extravagant,
inexhaustible grace is always extended to all—to whosoever
will—irrespective of background, past performance, or worthiness. Grace, by its very nature, is unmerited. It is radically consistent in this regard.

Nevertheless, even though grace is abundant and powerful, very
few benefit from it fully. Why? Because it is not enough for grace
to be offered; it must be *received*.

The Greek word translated "grace" in the New Testament is
charis—a word that carries a deeply embedded connotation of
"gift." And a gift, by definition, must be received. If you can earn
it, then what you are getting is a *wage*, not a gift. If you can win it,
it's a *prize*. If you can qualify for it, it's a *reward*.

This is why pride is such an obstacle to partaking of God's abundant grace. Pride prefers wages, prizes, and rewards. When a gift is offered to us, all we can do is either humbly receive it and be grateful, or refuse it.

We are saved "by grace through faith" (Ephesians 2:8 HCSB). Colossians 2:6 tells us, "So then, just as you received Christ Jesus as Lord, continue to live your lives in him." In other words, the only way to live the Christian life is the same way we began it—each day, simply receiving what God has for us with gratitude.

Grace is amazing, free, and consistent, but it cannot save you, empower you, or bless you as long as the gift remains unreceived. Unless you humbly choose to embrace the grace extended to you, it will remain an extended hand you've refused to grasp.

Prayer of Declaration

Father, I will not insult Your grace by treating Your extraordinary gift as a reward, prize, or wages earned. I lay aside my pride and humbly receive what You've freely offered.

Lord, I'm also grateful that You don't play favorites.

I declare that Your free, radically consistent gift of grace is fully and wholly available to me. I receive it! I receive grace for overcoming, for achieving, and for navigating the complexities and challenges of this day with supernatural peace and purpose. With a thankful heart, I take hold of Your extended hand. Your supernatural help and empowerment are mine today!

Active Waiting

"And he arose and came to his father.
But when he was still a great way off,
his father saw him and had compassion,
and ran and fell on his neck and kissed him."

LUKE 15:20 NKJV

What do you do when an answer to prayer seems slow in coming? How are you—the grace-conscious, faith-filled believer—supposed to respond when you've been standing on an unequivocal Bible promise that seems no closer to manifesting today than when you first took your stand?

First, it's vital that you not allow the seeming delay to erode your confidence in the goodness and faithfulness of God. God isn't the problem. In Jesus, He lovingly made provision for your rescue and deliverance long before your crisis. He has already accomplished everything needed for your victory.

The Bible speaks frequently of waiting on the Lord. However, it is vital to understand that this sort of waiting is not passive, defeatist, or lethargic. For the grace-conscious person, there is active waiting. That might sound like a contradiction, but it isn't.

A well-known parable of Jesus offers us a beautiful example of this active kind of waiting. In the story of the prodigal, the foolish, wayward son finally decides to head home. The father sees his son coming while he is still a great way off (see Luke 15:20). Why was that? It was because the father was *actively waiting* for his son. He was hopefully and expectantly scanning the horizon because he was confident in his heart that his son would return.

This kind of hopeful expectancy characterizes active waiting upon the Lord.

In 1896, a great man of prayer, Andrew Murray, wrote, "Yes, it is wonderful when a waiting soul and a waiting God meet each other ... and, since His waiting is filled with nothing but goodness and graciousness, let ours be filled with nothing but rejoicing in that goodness, and a confident expectancy of that grace."

PRAYER OF DECLARATION

Lord, I actively wait upon You and upon the manifestation of Your gracious provision in my life. I acknowledge with gratitude that You've already done the great work on my behalf. Now I look with hope and expectancy for the fulfillment of all that Your Word promises. I rest in Your goodness. I draw comfort from Your faithfulness.

I declare confidently that You are accomplishing all that concerns me. You're moving and working for my good in the unseen realm of the spirit. You're even already in my future preparing days of purpose, fruitfulness, and blessing for me in Your great love. I'm at peace and rest but scanning the horizon because I know good things are on the way.

From Ownership to Possession

"See, I have placed the land before you; go in and possess the land which the Lord swore to give to your fathers ... So we took possession of this land at that time."

DEUTERONOMY 1:8, 3:12 NASB

By grace, God has already provided everything you need. Through the redemptive work of His Son, He has made provision for all the forgiveness, healing, finances, freedom, and overcoming power you will ever need. These things are yours. They belong to you; but as the children of Israel discovered, there is a critical difference between ownership and possession.

As the Israelite nation approached the Land of Promise, God spoke to them as a people and said, essentially, "It's yours. I give it to you. Now go take possession of it." The land became legally, judicially theirs the moment their mighty, sovereign God decreed it so. Yet nothing about their lives or circumstances changed in that moment.

In fact, an entire generation of Israelites died in the wilderness without ever enjoying what rightfully belonged to them. Why? Because they allowed fear and wrong belief to rob them of their God-given inheritance. Only Joshua, Caleb, and their families took possession of what that generation had been given. They moved into the land of blessing because they dared to believe that what God had said—"I give you this land"—was true.

Belief, or faith, is your extended hand to take possession of what God has already decreed is yours. Faith actually reaches over into the spiritual realm and draws what God has already supplied, then pulls it back into the physical realm: "on earth as in heaven." Understanding this will revolutionize your life.

PRAYER OF DECLARATION

Lord, I reach out to You right now in trust and confidence, so grateful for Your abundant grace. I reach out to lay hold of all You've already given me—starting with Your forgiveness of my sins, cleansing from my shame, and full restoration of my relationship to You. Then moving on to the manifold riches of life in You: healing, victory, joy, and purpose in Your service blessing others.

I declare today that I am not content to live in the wilderness when You've given me a Promised Land. Not only do I own it, I'm taking possession of it bit by bit, day by day, victory to victory!

A Relationship, Not a Transaction

If God is for us, who can be against us? He who did not spare his own Son,
but gave him up for us all—how will he not also, along with him,
graciously give us all things?

ROMANS 8:31–32 NIV

We've been programmed by our culture to think transaction-ally. Our language is filled with clichés and phrases that reflect our transactional nature: "You get what you pay for," "I scratch your back; you scratch mine," "No pain, no gain," "You'll only get out of it what you put into it."

The fact is, for many things in the natural world, these sayings are true and wise. Perhaps this is why we have such a hard time comprehending the grace of God. That's because our interactions with God are relational, not transactional.

That means *doing* more for God doesn't earn you more favor with Him. Nor does asking something big of Him require more deposits in some invisible account or more earned points on some heavenly tally sheet.

That's the definition of works: trying to earn God's favor or blessing by performing the right actions or behaviors. A works mode is the opposite of grace, and it's the wrong way to approach the Lord.

God is not a vending machine into which we insert an adequate amount of payment—right living, righteous behavior, prayer, witnessing—in order to extract something in return. What a relief! Jesus is the One who, in a single transaction, paid the enormous price to put us in direct *relationship* with God. Now everything we need flows from that Father-child relationship.

Yes, we pray and do good to others, we share our faith and do other good works, but we do all these things as a natural outflow of the relationship we already have securely, completely, and irrevocably with God. Our good works aren't a form of currency we use to pay for God's favor and help.

GOD IS NOT A VENDING MACHINE INTO WHICH WE INSERT AN ADEQUATE AMOUNT OF PAYMENT IN ORDER TO EXTRACT SOMETHING IN RETURN.

Prayer of Declaration

God, I am so grateful for the gift of relationship with You. It is almost too much for me to grasp. Forgive me when I slip back into approaching You transactionally, rather than relationally. I am so thankful that You are the kind of Father who wants to know me and abide with me, and You do not seek my performance, but rather my faith and love.

I love You, Heavenly Father. I love being in relationship with You. And, Your unconditional, irrevocable love and acceptance have freed me to let my light shine before others so they can see my good works and glorify You. I will not insult or demean Your grace by trying to buy Your favor or blessing. As Romans 8:32 says, since You have already lavishly given me Your Son, "how will You not also, along with Him, graciously give me all things?"

The Eyes of Your Heart

I pray that the eyes of your heart may be enlightened, so that you will know what is the hope of His calling, what are the riches of the glory of His inheritance in the saints, and what is the surpassing greatness of His power toward us who believe.

EPHESIANS 1:18–19 NASB

On several occasions, Jesus spoke of people who have eyes to see, and ears to hear, and of others who did not. He clearly wasn't referring to literal eyes and ears, as almost everyone to whom He was speaking had a functioning set of eyeballs and eardrums.

No, He was speaking of the ability to see and hear spiritual truth. Spiritual reality. Just as our natural senses help us understand and navigate the natural world, we have spiritual senses that do the same for us in the spiritual realm. The apostle Paul had this in mind when he wrote to the believers in Ephesus.

A newborn baby's eyes contain all the power they will ever need, but they reveal very little to the baby's mind. That's because the infant's mind hasn't been trained. It doesn't know what to look for or how to interpret what it sees.

In a similar way, the eyes of your heart may be equally untrained and immature, but those eyes exist all the same. And what they're looking at is every bit as real as the big, wide world around that bewildered newborn. In the spirit, there is a whole world in which joy, peace, healing, provision, and favor have already been purchased for you. You'd know your name is written upon each gift if only you could see them.

That is precisely why Paul prayed as he did in Ephesians, chapter one. He knew we need to have our spiritual eyes enlightened in order to clearly see all that God has made available to us in Christ. Paul says we need those illuminated eyes so we can know the hope of His calling, the riches of the glory of His inheritance in the saints, and the surpassing greatness of His power toward believers like us.

YOU'D KNOW YOUR NAME IS WRITTEN UPON EACH GIFT IF ONLY YOU COULD SEE THEM.

PRAYER OF DECLARATION

Father, I cannot lay hold of what I cannot see. It is hard to follow a path I cannot perceive. So, I come into agreement with Paul's prayer.

Thank You for opening the eyes of my heart to see the things of the Spirit—to glimpse the reality of all You've delivered for me today. I see more clearly the hope of Your calling and the riches of the glory of Your inheritance in me. You're opening my eyes daily to the truth about the overwhelming greatness of Your power and love toward me.

I declare that my heart is seeing more clearly every day! And whatever I see, I lay hold of in faith.

One Foundational Assumption

Taste and see that the Lord is good.
Oh, the joys of those who take refuge in him!

PSALM 34:8 NLT

Life in this broken, fallen world is filled with mysteries. There is much we don't understand concerning suffering, injustice, pain, and heartache. Theologians and philosophers have wrestled for centuries with the problem of evil.

Sorting out and reconciling the tensions between the biblical concepts of God's sovereignty, man's free will, and how the fall of man distorted nature is a challenge for another day. However, it's vital that we settle one particular question in our hearts. In fact, the very foundation of our capacity to receive from God relies upon an unshakeable confidence in this one truth:

He is good!

One of the most ancient and oft-repeated songs of praise in the Old Testament is this one:

> *Oh, give thanks to the Lord, for He is good! For His mercy endures forever.*

These words occur, with slight variations, in 1 Chronicles 16:34, 2 Chronicles 5:13, Ezra 3:11, and several different places in the book of Psalms. Do you think that perhaps they are important to our understanding of God?

The foundational truth of our faith is that God's goodness is infinite and absolute. And it was on full display the day He offered up His own Son to not only die *for*, but also to die *as* us. Don't ever doubt it. When life or circumstances don't seem to make sense, question everything before you question this: God is good. He is for you. If you are ever tempted to doubt it, look to the cross.

The 19th century British theologian Charles Kingsley said it this way: "Whatever may be the mysteries of life and death, there is one mystery which the cross of Christ reveals to us, and that is the infinite and absolute goodness of God."

PRAYER OF DECLARATION

Father God, please give me a deeper, fuller revelation of Your character and kindness. Help me see the cross as Your magnificent, redemptive love on display. Anchor my trust in Your kindness and care so deeply that it can never be shaken. Thank You for Your everlasting, inexhaustible mercy.

I declare that You are good to me and Your mercies are new every morning. I will question everything before I question Your kindness toward me. You are for me. You want only what is best for me. I have tasted and seen that You are good; so I joyfully take refuge in You.

Look Into the Face of Love

Enter his gates with thanksgiving; go into his courts with praise. Give thanks to him and praise his name. For the Lord is good. His unfailing love continues forever, and his faithfulness continues to each generation.

PSALM 100:4–5 NLT

One of the most famous sermons of the prerevolutionary era in America is the Puritan preacher Jonathan Edwards' message titled, "Sinners in the Hands of an Angry God." Contemporary accounts indicate it was highly effective in getting lost people to come to God, and almost equally effective at getting Christians to question whether or not they were truly converted.

In other words, the sermon is famous for being terrifying.

There are many strains of Christianity that seem to delight in portraying God as a fierce, wrathful Judge-King searching for reasons to disqualify His subjects from receiving any of His blessings while simultaneously watching for opportunities to dole out punishments.

Here is wonderful news: the ruler who sits upon the throne of the universe is neither a cruel tyrant nor an angry, vindictive monarch demanding to be appeased. He is, above all, a Father—a *good* Father—and as such finds great joy in blessing His children. He longs to show us favor and delights in our well-being.

When blood-washed believers approach that glorious throne and look into the face of the mighty One, they find nothing but perfect love there.

Andrew Murray, the amazing missionary to South Africa and deep man of prayer, once wrote: "Look up and see our great God upon His throne. He is Love—and filled with an unceasing and inexpressible desire to communicate His goodness and blessedness to all His creatures. He longs and delights to bless."

It's true. God's wrath against sin has been spent. It was poured out upon His own Son at the cross.

PRAYER OF DECLARATION

Father, I thank You that You are love personified and that You delight in blessing me. You have opened the eyes and ears of my spirit and reveal Your goodness to me. So, I enter Your throne room joyfully and with a heart filled with gratitude.

I declare today that when I look into Your face, I see love, acceptance, and kindness there. I worship You. And I make my requests known to You in confidence. You are good. Your unfailing love and unwavering faithfulness continue forever, from generation to generation.

Our Fallible, Foolable Natural Senses

So he answered, "Do not fear, for those who are with us are more than those who are with them." And Elisha prayed, and said, "Lord, I pray, open his eyes that he may see." Then the Lord opened the eyes of the young man, and he saw.

2 KINGS 6:16—17 NKJV

Most people in the world have a vague sense that there is more to life—more to this world, to existence, to their own selves—than what they can see, taste, hear, smell, and feel. Even so, believers can spend the bulk of their days focused solely on what their senses are reporting, hardly giving a thought to the fact that much more may be going on unseen all around them.

Our senses are easily fooled. Our eyes can literally deceive us.

When we focus only on what our senses tell us, we're like the servant of the prophet Elisha who woke up to the sight of enemy armies lining the hillsides all around them and panicked. Elisha's helper thought the prophet was crazy for being calm ... right up to the moment his spiritual eyes were opened.

Only then could he see the overwhelming multitude of angelic help that was present to fight on their behalf. You see, our natural senses never tell us the whole truth.

That's why the grace-minded person isn't lying, in denial, or engaging in wishful thinking when he or she declares something that appears to be at odds with the available natural evidence. The grace-minded believer simply knows that the natural evidence is not *all* the evidence. In fact, he or she knows that the natural evidence is actually *less* reliable and more transient than the spiritual realities defined by God's Word.

As you pray, keep in mind that the natural world bends to the authority of the spiritual. This principle is at the root of every miracle recorded in the Bible. If, like Elisha, you believe, speak, and act on spiritual truth as revealed by the Spirit, it will transform the physical. Your unshakeable faith in God and His Word causes the wayward physical realm to change and come into conformity with all He's done in the spiritual.

PRAYER OF DECLARATION

Holy Spirit of God, keep me mindful as I move through my days that there is far more going on around me than my natural senses can perceive. Help me to glimpse and understand the spiritual truth and realities in every circumstance. I esteem and trust Your Word more highly than my fallible, foolable senses.

I declare today that the power that is for me is far greater than my enemy. Those who are with me far outnumber those who are against me. I do not rely solely on what my natural senses observe. I don't evaluate my circumstances only on what I see. Your Word and Your Spirit bring me to a higher, more reliable understanding of the truth.

Where Supernatural Power Blooms

But [the Lord] said to me, "My grace is sufficient for you, for my power is made perfect in weakness." Therefore I will boast all the more gladly of my weaknesses, so that the power of Christ may rest upon me.

2 CORINTHIANS 12:9 ESV

So much of the way the Kingdom of God works is counterintuitive to the natural mind. This is particularly true where grace is concerned. To the world's way of thinking it all seems upside down and backwards. But in reality, it is this fallen world's thinking that is upside down.

The apostle Paul's infamous thorn in the flesh in 2 Corinthians 12 is a great example. This passage has been cited frequently to justify some people's misguided, very destructive belief that God puts sickness or pain on His children. This, of course, ignores Paul's direct statement that his thorn was a messenger from Satan.

After praying three times for this weakness to be removed, the Lord spoke to Paul. A fair and faithful unpacking of the original Greek of 2 Corinthians 12:9 would be:

My grace is all you need, because the gift of My supernatural power blooms in the places where you realize you are weak. "My enablement rushes in to fill the gaps where you acknowledge you cannot do it in your own strength."

This is an enormous, little-understood key to living a life of power and victory: a grace life! The more we recognize that we need Jesus in every moment for everything, the more power becomes available to us. But when we put our trust in our own human abilities and efforts, we leave little room for God's gift of power to move in. Prideful self-reliance and self-regard neutralize grace!

PRAYER OF DECLARATION

Father, I recognize how completely helpless and needy I am in my own strength. I recognize that what Jesus said is true. I am merely a branch grafted into a magnificent Vine.

I declare that apart from Jesus I can do nothing. I happily acknowledge my need for You. I receive the gift of Your supernatural power to fill the large and numerous gaps in my ability and strength. I humbly accept Your grace and supernatural empowerment. I am happy to be dependent upon You.

Today, the gift of Your supernatural power will bloom in my weakness. Your enablement is rushing in to fill the gaps where I know I cannot do it in my own strength. Your grace is sufficient for me.

Choose the Right Covenant

It is not that we think we are qualified to do anything on our own. Our qualification comes from God. He has enabled us to be ministers of his new covenant. ... If the old way, which brings condemnation, was glorious, how much more glorious is the new way, which makes us right with God!

2 CORINTHIANS 3:5–6, 9 NLT

Old Testament. New Testament.

Even the very structure of our Bibles shouts that God's glorious story of redemption is broken into two great phases or eras. The Old Covenant era was necessary in order to get the Savior—the Messiah—into the world. Once that was accomplished, His sacrificial death became the centerpiece of a new and "better covenant, based on better promises" (Hebrews 8:6–8 NKJV). Quickly, the old one became obsolete (see Hebrews 8:13).

In the verses above, Paul is reminding us that the old covenant brought condemnation. This was actually by God's design. A key role of the Law was to keep mankind aware that we needed that promised Savior! And, when that Savior came, the new covenant in His blood dealt with condemnation once and for all.

If you are consistently feeling condemned in your relationship to God, it is likely that you are trying to live under the wrong covenant. When you entered into the new and better covenant by being born again, you were gifted Jesus' righteousness and right standing with God. No wonder the Gospel is truthfully called *Good News*!

But sadly, many believers have not renewed their minds to the reality of what Paul declared in Romans 8:1 (NKJV): "There is therefore now no condemnation for those who are in Christ Jesus." As a result, they fail to experience many of the wonderful benefits of living under the New Covenant.

They live in confusion, doubt, and fear—clinging to shreds of the Law and grasping at threads of grace.

Don't live this way! Begin today to renew your mind to the glorious new reality that you are right with God, not by virtue of your performance or behavior, but by the superior virtue of Jesus' flawless life.

Prayer of Declaration

Father, I am well aware that I am not qualified to do anything on my own. But I rejoice that my qualification comes through Jesus and His blood that sealed this new, better covenant.

I declare today that I am a minister of this covenant. I am right with God. Condemnation has no place in my mind or heart. The new covenant in Jesus' blood dealt with condemnation once and for all. And in Him, I qualify for all the better promises this glorious new covenant provides. I qualify for healing, provision, and everything Jesus died to provide.

Slaying Your Goliaths

What, then, shall we say in response to these things?
If God is for us, who can be against us? ...
No, in all these things we are more than conquerors
through him who loved us.

ROMANS 8:31, 37 NIV

When you think about the day ahead, what taunting, boasting enemies do you hear calling to you, trying to instill fear in your heart? Are there some big, seemingly invincible adversaries standing between you and the breakthroughs you long for?

If so, you probably wish you had bold, David-like faith to confidently run at and slay those Goliaths. If your faith is not what you wish it to be, perhaps your understanding of who you are in Christ needs some fine-tuning. It is possible that you are listening to voices that are directing your focus away from King Jesus and onto yourself.

Sadly, many well-meaning and sincere teachers, preachers, and "spiritual" family members do not have an accurate understanding of God's amazing grace, or the utter completeness and finality of Jesus' finished work on the cross. It does, indeed, seem too good to be true, but that is why the Bible calls it Good News!

You have a choice today. Your attention can focus on

1. Your Goliaths: the biggest problems you currently face

2. Yourself: your weakness, failings, limitations, and past mistakes

3. Your Savior: His power, might, perfection, goodness, and compassion toward you

Choose option three. The more you focus on Jesus—His words, actions, and role in God's plan of redemption—the more your faith and confidence soar. Diligently guard your heart. Disregard or avoid voices and messages that urge you to put your focus on yourself or your challenges. Instead, spend time with the words of Jesus and let His glory and grace fill your heart with confidence.

PRAYER OF DECLARATION

Father, since You are for me, who can be against me? Please give me discernment and wisdom concerning what voices I allow to speak into my mind and heart. My own strength and abilities are irrelevant. The size of any problems I face right now shrink to insignificance in comparison to Your might.

I declare that I am in You, Jesus, and You are in me. My eyes are on You. I'm focusing on Your power, might, perfection, goodness, and compassion toward me. And these things fill me with bold, David-like faith to confidently run at and slay my Goliaths today.

Secure in His Hands,
Blessed in His Truth

"I give them eternal life, and they shall never perish; no one will snatch them
out of my hand. My Father, who has given them to me, is greater than all;
no one can snatch them out of my Father's hand."

JOHN 10:28–29 NIV

Your enemy—who you may remember Jesus called "the father of lies"—loves to try and rob you of the joy and confidence of your salvation. In fact, since Jesus stripped him of his authority through His victory over death, lies are the only remaining weapon in the devil's arsenal. Another word for this weapon is "deception."

The only way Satan can rob you is to get you to use your own God-granted power and authority against yourself by getting you to believe a lie. What you believe (or misbelieve) has an enormous impact on your quality of life and circumstances.

One of the most common of these lies is the notion that you should live in ongoing fear of God's judgment. That God may become so annoyed with your mistakes and failings, that He may eventually abandon you or reject you altogether, or, at minimum, that God still waits to pounce on you in condemnation and punishing wrath. Nothing could be further from the truth.

Jesus made it clear: When you repent of your sins and place your faith in Him, you are forever His and nothing—including your own human frailty and fallibility—can remove you from His hand. You have passed from death to life and out of the fear of judgment forever. That holy fire fell completely on our Lord at Golgotha.

Under the Old Covenant, when a worshipper brought a lamb to the tabernacle to be sacrificed, the priest did not examine the worshipper in order to determine whether he or she was worthy. No, he examined the lamb, to ensure the sacrifice was perfect and unblemished. Jesus was and is your perfect, faultless Lamb, sacrificed to secure your forgiveness and adoption.

No, the enemy can't have you. But he can prevent you from enjoying everything Jesus purchased for you by getting you to believe a lie.

WHAT YOU BELIEVE HAS AN ENORMOUS IMPACT ON YOUR QUALITY OF LIFE AND CIRCUMSTANCES.

PRAYER OF DECLARATION

Father, I thank You that according to Colossians 1:13, my legal ownership and residence has been transferred out of the domain of darkness and into the kingdom of Your beloved Son.

I declare that I belong to You, and nothing, not even my own periodic foolishness, can remove me from Your mighty loving hand. This is settled forever. You will never leave me nor forsake me. You are faithful even when I am faithless. I am secure and at rest, and therefore free to follow wherever You lead.

I guard my heart and mind from deception by reading, pondering, and proclaiming aloud Your Word of truth.

The Power of a Clean Conscience

Since we have a great priest over the house of God, let us draw near with
a true heart in full assurance of faith, with our hearts sprinkled clean
from an evil conscience and our bodies washed with pure water.

Hebrews 10:21–22 esv

Have you ever wondered if you must fully confess each and every sin you commit every day in order to be truly righteous and clean before God? Have you been taught that it is important to provide a detailed, itemized accounting of every time you have missed the mark before you can even think about fellowshipping with God or, heaven forbid, asking Him for anything?

It isn't true. It was your confession and repentant agreement that you are a sinner that released God's gracious forgiveness when you were born again.

Don't misunderstand; confession of sins is a healthy and worthy spiritual practice. It is a vital help in maintaining your heart confidence before God. If your conscience is not clear, confess it, *knowing forgiveness is already yours.* But it is not about scouring your memory for every last scrap of failure and omission.

Think of your confession as a soul-baring, heart-cleansing talk with a loving Father. He already knows you better than you know yourself.

Then, knowing your conscience has been sprinkled clean of guilt and condemnation by Jesus' blood, you can have total boldness and confidence to enter God's holy presence, offering a heart wholly devoted to Him.

PRAYER OF DECLARATION

Lord, I am so grateful that the forgiveness You offer me is not dependent on my perfect ability to confess every sin. My cleansing depends instead on the power of Jesus' cleansing blood that was shed at Calvary. Thank You for the peace and joy it brings me to know and acknowledge this. What a relief, Heavenly Father!

I declare that today I will have boldness and confidence to enter Your presence and usher Your Spirit into every corner of my heart. My conscience has been cleansed, not because of the perfection of my repentance but because of the perfection of Jesus' sacrifice and God's inexhaustible mercy.

The Power of Heart Confidence

This is how we...set our hearts at rest in his presence: If our hearts condemn us,
we know that God is greater than our hearts, and he knows everything.
Dear friends, if our hearts do not condemn us, we have confidence
before God and receive from him anything we ask.

1 JOHN 3:19—22 NIV

This passage reveals a powerful, frequently misunderstood spiritual principle; namely, that your ability to receive from God is directly tied to the level of confidence in your heart as you approach Him in prayer.

If you come to God with your heart condemning you, it is very difficult for you to receive what God has already willingly provided. If you come to Him feeling unworthy, disqualified, and judged because of your mistakes and failings, your receiver is severely limited and possibly broken entirely!

But if, on the other hand, you approach God boldly and confidently because you know you're coming not on your own merits but in Jesus' merits and His righteousness, your receiver is big and fully functional.

The goal is to have your heart at rest in His presence. This should be your natural state any time you approach your Heavenly Father. But if it's not, there is good news for you: "God is greater than your heart." He knows everything about you and loves you anyway.

As you prepare to come to the Lord, do a quick heart check. Is it condemning you? Do you feel even the slightest twinge of reluctance or hesitance about coming before God's throne of grace?

If so, just take that as a signal to put yourself back into full remembrance that you are not coming in your own righteousness. You have Jesus' righteousness because He took your sinfulness upon Himself. Is the Holy Spirit bringing some habit, practice, or attitude to your attention? Then correct and adjust, and keep moving forward, toward your loving Heavenly Father!

Remember that you are in Him. In fact, according to Galatians 3:27, you have been "clothed" with Him.

The key to receiving in prayer is understanding the principle of heart confidence.

YOUR ABILITY TO RECEIVE FROM GOD IS DIRECTLY TIED TO THE LEVEL OF CONFIDENCE IN YOUR HEART.

Prayer of Declaration

Father, I am clothed in Your beloved Son and therefore come to You confidently. I am not coming in my own righteousness. I have Jesus' righteousness because He took my sinfulness upon Himself. You know everything about me—my darkest secrets and my worst impulses—and You love me anyway.

I declare, therefore, that because Jesus is my righteousness, my heart does not condemn me. No, it is at rest in Your wonderful, loving presence. And because my heart does not condemn me, I know I have and receive all that I ask as well as all that belongs to me in Jesus.

Comprehensive Salvation

For I am not ashamed of the gospel, for it is the power of God for salvation to everyone who believes, to the Jew first and also to the Greek.

ROMANS 1:16 ESV

The word "salvation" has been used with such routine regularity in evangelical circles that its meaning has both narrowed and thinned in our ears. It has lost its power. If we understood the full breadth and depth of what it means to be saved, our hearts would thrill at every mention of the word.

For the typical believer, salvation means, more than anything else, a ticket to heaven. Being saved means going to heaven when you die.

Of course, the assurance of spending eternity enjoying God's love and exploring the endless depths of His goodness is a blessing beyond description! If this alone was all salvation delivered for the believer, it would still be the greatest gift ever given— doubly so when one ponders that it also means avoiding the horrific reality of eternity separated from God.

But salvation has enormous implications for today, in this life, as well. And setting the record straight about this word is the key to unlocking all the power Jesus came to give you—power you might find lacking in your life today.

Behind the word "salvation" in our English Bibles is the deeply rich Greek word *soteria*, which carries the meaning "rescue, deliverance from enemies, preservation, and safety." God sent Jesus to rescue you from sin and its fatal consequences, and to deliver you from every work and attack of the enemy, including, sickness, oppression, depression, confusion, purposelessness, and poverty.

As Paul told the Galatians, "Christ redeemed us from the curse of the Law, *having become* a curse for us"(Galatians 3:13 NASB). Salvation means deliverance, rescue, and safety from every aspect of the curse—not just in the next life, but in this life, too.

PRAYER OF DECLARATION

God, I rejoice that heaven is my future eternal home. What a gift! And, I also thank You that my soteria began the moment I was born again.

I declare that by faith, and in the authority that is mine in Jesus, I walk in the fulness of that deliverance today. No aspect of the curse—no attack of the enemy—has a place in my life. I overcome. I rise above. I come through unscathed. Rescue, deliverance, preservation, provision, and safety are mine. I have been utterly, gloriously, completely, and eternally saved.

The Healing-Forgiveness Connection

Jesus knew what they were thinking, so he asked them, "Why do you have such evil thoughts in your hearts? Is it easier to say 'Your sins are forgiven,' or 'Stand up and walk'? So I will prove to you that the Son of Man has the authority on earth to forgive sins." Then Jesus turned to the paralyzed man and said, "Stand up, pick up your mat, and go home!"

MATTHEW 9:4–6 NLT

A small but significant percentage of Christians struggle to receive and accept God's forgiveness. For whatever reason, they think what they have done is too awful or their sins are too numerous. They know that God can and does forgive others but that somehow they are beyond the reach of His mercy.

But this is not the norm. Most believers have little trouble accepting that God is able to forgive them of their sins, and that He has indeed done so. However, many of these same Christians struggle to really believe that God will heal them. They will tell you that God can and does heal people, but they can muster no confidence that He will heal *them*.

Perhaps you are among them. If so, consider the story of the paralyzed man whose friends lowered him through a roof to hear Jesus speak. As the Scripture reference reveals, Jesus first told the man that his sins were forgiven. This offended many religious leaders in the crowd, and Jesus knew it.

The Savior asked the leaders, "Which is easier: forgiving sin or healing a broken body?" Jesus' question carried two implications: First, anyone with the God-given authority to raise up a lame man also has the authority to forgive sin; and second, that sin and sickness are linked. That is to say, sickness came into the world as a result of sin. The world's sickness problem is rooted in the world's sin problem.

The clear and vital message for us is that Jesus dealt with both sin and sickness on the cross. Our sins were laid upon Him (see Isaiah 53:4), He became a curse for us (see Galatians 3:13), and by His stripes we were healed (see 1 Peter 2:24).

Thus, healing is just as much a part of the atonement as is forgiveness of sin. A clear conscience and sound body belong to you. For God, one is no harder than the other.

THE CLEAR AND VITAL MESSAGE FOR US IS THAT JESUS DEALT WITH BOTH SIN AND SICKNESS ON THE CROSS.

PRAYER OF DECLARATION

Father, I accept and rejoice that forgiveness and healing were both abundantly provided through Jesus' extraordinary sacrifice on the cross. Because of this, I know I am never beyond the reach of Your mercy or healing power.

With the Psalmist I declare, "Bless You, Lord! I will forget none of Your benefits. You have pardoned all my sins. You have healed all my diseases." It is no harder for You to heal me than it is for You to forgive me. Jesus made provision for both in His sacrificial death and resurrection. Thank You!

The Opposite of Fear

There is no fear in love, but perfect love casts out fear. For fear has to do with punishment, and whoever fears has not been perfected in love.

1 JOHN 4:18 ESV

"The only thing we have to fear is fear itself," President Franklin D. Roosevelt famously said at his inauguration, during the depths of America's Great Depression. The concept he was trying to convey has meaning for us today in areas far beyond the realms of economics or government. His point was that fear is often its own self-fulfilling prophecy.

Fear is a spiritual force that can actually attract the very things it dreads. In a sense, it is the opposite of faith. Faith is positive expectancy of good from God. Fear is negative expectancy. As such, it shuts down your capacity to receive from God. What a hellish prison it is to live in fear. At a spiritual level, fear paralyzes and prevents you from fulfilling God's unique, amazing destiny for you.

As anyone who has battled it can tell you, fear doesn't respond to reason. You can't simply tell a fear-filled person to just stop being fearful. Providing facts and arguments is futile. A spiritual condition can't be fixed by feeding the mind. It can only be eradicated by a Spirit-encounter with love personified.

This is why Paul prayed for his friends in Ephesus, "That you, being rooted and established in love, may have power, together with all the Lord's holy people, to grasp how wide and long and high and deep is the love of Christ, and to know this love that surpasses knowledge—that you may be filled to the measure of all the fullness of God" (Ephesians 3:17–19 NIV).

The more you immerse yourself and anchor your heart in the truth of Jesus' boundless, unconditional love for you, the less fear plays a part in your life.

FEAR IS THE OPPOSITE OF FAITH.
FAITH IS POSITIVE EXPECTANCY
OF GOOD FROM GOD.

PRAYER OF DECLARATION

Dear God, by Your Spirit, grace me with a fresh revelation of Your love for me. I come into agreement with Paul's Ephesians 3 prayer. Let the knowledge of Your boundless, unconditional love for me drive any and all remnants of fear from my soul—filling me with the fullness of You.

I declare that I am rooted and grounded in Your love. I immerse myself and anchor my heart in the truth of Jesus' unconditional love for me. I expect only good, not evil. You, the God of the universe, have placed Your covenant love upon me. I am encircled with the strong, loving arms of a perfect Father. The Lord is my light and my salvation. Whom shall I fear?

No Condemnation

*"For God did not send His Son into the world to condemn the world,
but that the world through Him might be saved."*

JOHN 3:17 NKJV

You may be surprised to learn that the devil has a ministry. His is a *ministry of condemnation*. One of his titles in the Word of God is "accuser of the brethren" (Revelation 12:10 NKJV).

Something amazing happens when you truly realize, deep down, that you are saved utterly and forever by simple grace through faith, and that your works and worthiness have nothing to do with it. Really *knowing* this frees you from that tired, old ministry of condemnation and the deadly baggage that comes with it: guilt, insecurity, dread, anxiety, and fears of every kind.

Condemnation steals your peace. It robs you of the joy of your relationship with your Father. It drains you of your confidence before God, which determines your capacity to receive His blessings and promises.

The wonderful news is that "There is therefore now no condemnation to those who are in Christ Jesus" (Romans 8:1 NKJV). This is true for you unless you allow the enemy to operate his ministry of condemnation in your life when he has no right or place to do so. You have been given the righteousness of Jesus Christ for all time.

Oh, what a wonderful way to live!

When you truly believe that you're no longer under condemnation, and that your Father-child relationship with God is founded upon a new and better covenant of grace, you approach your heavenly Father willingly and cast your every care upon Him. Remember, He has actually asked to carry the burden for all your troubles and worries. You can cast your cares upon Him today because He cares for you.

If you are feeling condemnation today, its source is not your heavenly Father.

Prayer of Declaration

Jesus, because of You, I no longer live under the yoke of condemnation and shame. I will not allow the accuser to operate his ministry of condemnation in my heart and mind.

I declare that I reject the enemy's ministry of condemnation that steals my peace, robs my joy, and drains my confidence before You. I live today and every day under Your Spirit's ministry of righteousness, life, and liberty.

I am saved forever by grace through faith. My relationship with You is founded upon a new and better covenant of grace. Therefore, I cast my cares upon You today, Father, resting in the wonderful knowledge that You care for me.

What God Has Declared Clean

The voice spoke to him a second time:
"Stop treating as unclean what God has made clean."
Acts 10:15 cjb

Very early in the life of the Church, the apostle Peter had a remarkable vision that completely altered the course of Christian history. In Acts 10, we read how the former fisherman was praying on a rooftop when he saw heaven opened and a sheet descending before him. On that sheet were many animals that the Levitical dietary laws declared unclean.

As a devout Jewish follower of Jesus, Peter instantly recognized these creatures as forbidden and defiling to even touch. Thus, he was shocked to hear a voice from heaven commanding him to kill and eat them! Of course, Peter protested.

In response, the voice of the Lord issued a command to Peter: "What God has cleansed, no longer consider unholy" (Acts 10:15 NASB).

The Spirit of God could very well say the same thing to us today. Ask the typical believer if he or she is holy, and you will likely get a weak, half-hearted, disclaimer-laden response that ranges somewhere between, "Not exactly," and, "Oh, heavens, no!"

Ask believers if they think they are pure, and the responses will be similarly sheepish. These answers are in spite of the fact that the Word of God is clear and unequivocal that if you are in Christ, God has declared you holy, clean, and pure.

God has declared you righteous. Follow the command that He issued to Peter: stop calling unclean what He has declared holy.

PRAYER OF DECLARATION

Father, forgive me for ever calling unclean that which You have declared clean. Thank You for the complete cleansing I experienced through the blood of Jesus. By Your grace, help me renew my mind and realign my thinking to this reality. I reject the condemning voice of the accuser.

I declare that I am holy, chosen, purified, cleansed, and set apart for Your service and delight. I joyfully concur with Hebrews 10:10 that by Your will, I have been made holy through the sacrifice of the body of Jesus Christ, once and for all!

Righteousness and Restitution

Zacchaeus joyously welcomed Jesus and was amazed over his gracious visit to his home. Zacchaeus stood in front of the Lord and said, "Half of all that I own I will give to the poor. And Lord, if I have cheated anyone, I promise to pay back four times as much as I stole."

Luke 19:8 TPT

Renewing our minds to the truth that in Christ we are wholly and completely made righteous with His righteousness is a process that takes time. We don't unlearn a lifetime of religious condemnation, fear, and shame overnight.

Along the way on that journey, many believers encounter a question: *What about those who have been harmed by my past sin? What of those I have wronged in the past?* We wonder, *To be truly forgiven and put in right-standing with God, isn't it necessary for me to go and try to make right those wrongs?*

Of course, there are past actions that injured others for which no restitution is humanly possible. What's done can't ever be undone. However, certain other kinds of actions, such as defrauding someone of money, can possibly be made right.

The fact is, both categories of sin were placed upon Jesus on the cross; the guilt and shame associated with it were wholly and fully borne by Him. As far as our right-standing with God is concerned, there can be no difference between the two.

However, our intimate fellowship with God may very well produce in us a desire to make restitution where restitution is possible. The perfect biblical example of this is Zacchaeus. The corrupt tax collector had defrauded many people of money. However, it's vital to note that Jesus did not make restitution a condition of fellowship with Him. Jesus did not say, "You've cheated people. If you'll go make that right, then I'll come to your house and dine with you."

No, Zacchaeus's desire to make restitution emerged organically and spontaneously in his heart *after* being accepted and embraced by Jesus.

Intimacy with God—which is only possible when we embrace the truth that we have the complete righteousness of Jesus—will always produce godly desires (like the desire to make restitution) that we should act upon. But we must be on guard against stepping over into works by viewing those acts as a *condition* of fellowship or acceptance, rather than as an outgrowth of the acceptance we already have.

Like everything else in the realm of God's grace, we operate *from* what Jesus has already accomplished.

Prayer of Declaration

Father, You declared me righteous the instant I surrendered my life to Christ and accepted His sacrifice on my behalf. Thank You!

Jesus, I thank You that You didn't leave me as I was. I've learned that being in Your presence changes me, filling me with the desire and power to change from the inside out.

I declare that my connection to God through Jesus produces godly desires within me, and that I'm acting upon those desires. I'm quick to respond to promptings from Your Spirit. And when Your Spirit prompts me to make restitution, seek forgiveness, or seek reconciliation, I'm quick to do so.

Your Father's Love

See what an incredible quality of love the Father has shown to us, that we would [be permitted to] be named and called and counted the children of God! And so we are!

1 John 3:1 AMP

Well-fathered children tend to do better in life. That's the clear picture that is emerging in our increasingly fatherless culture.

What kind of earthly father did you have? Did you grow up with a loving and wonderful daddy? If so, you were blessed indeed. Most fathers are as flawed and broken as the rest of us; they fall far short of the ideal. Far too many children today grow up with no father at all.

Whatever your situation might have been growing up, your experience does not have to be your only chance at a loving relationship as the child of a wonderful father.

When you have a clear and complete picture of God's immense love for you, you can approach Him not through the Law's fear and trembling, but through the loving invitation of a Father who longs to spend time with His kid. You can enjoy all the access and intimacy with Him you've longed for in a father, knowing it's not only allowed, it's desired!

This intimacy has the power to bring forth good fruit in your life and usher in the victory you need today. Whatever challenge or enemy you need to defeat—fear of death, rejection, failure, the hurt of a broken relationship, or the bondage of an addiction—you can overcome it through the freely-given power of your heavenly Father, who wants you to win as much as you do.

You are a well-Fathered child. When you bask in the glory of God's all-powerful love and amazing grace, you can't help but thrive.

PRAYER OF DECLARATION

Papa God, thank You for breaking through the fog of my fearful thinking and giving me a clear picture of Your true love for me. What an incredible quality of love it is. I confidently, joyfully engage You today in conversation and communion—not formally but intimately. I engage You as a child would a kind and perfect Father.

I declare that I am a well-Fathered child. Your Fatherly love is transforming me from the inside out. Therefore, I triumph over every enemy through the freely-given power of Your Spirit within me. Your Spirit testifies to my spirit that I am indeed Your child.

Love Fulfills the Law

Love makes it impossible to harm another,
so love fulfills all that the law requires.
ROMANS 13:10 TPT

For fifteen centuries following the giving of the Law on Mt. Sinai, the Israelite tribes strived, strained, and struggled to fulfill its requirements, but they failed. We now know that their failure was foreknown and preordained by God. As the apostle Paul makes clear in several of his letters, the hidden purpose of the Law was to make us aware that we were hopelessly, helplessly sinful and in need of a Savior (see Romans 3:20; Galatians 3:19).

However, by the time Jesus arrived, there were some in Israel who had actually convinced themselves that they were keeping the Law fully. Remember the rich young ruler? When Jesus asked him about the requirements of the Law the young man replied, "All these things I have kept from my youth" (see Luke 18:21). Spoiler alert: *He hadn't.*

Then came Jesus: He perfectly fulfilled every requirement of the Law as mankind's proxy or substitute. At the same time, He declared that the totality of the Law was actually encapsulated in two simple instructions: "Love God. Love people" (see Matthew 22:36-40).

This is the extraordinary thing about Jesus' love for us. It not only frees us from the condemnation of the Law, but actually *fulfills* it! Of course, consistently walking in that kind of love is still beyond the reach of fallen, broken people apart from God. But here's wonderful news: Romans 5:5 (NKJV) declares, "The love of God has been poured out in our hearts by the Holy Spirit who was given to us." It's in there! All we have to do is simply yield to it.

When you have Christ's love inside you, you can't help but fulfill the Law. It comes naturally, without coercion, compulsion, or striving. Your heart overflows with grace and lovingkindness, leaving you no desire to engage in those destructive behaviors called sin.

God's love in you and working through you naturally accomplishes what our frantic, fruitless striving cannot.

PRAYER OF DECLARATION

Father, thank You for Your extraordinary love. I recognize that when I embrace Your love and let it flow through me, I naturally, organically do all that Your perfect Law demanded.

I declare that Your supernatural love has been poured out to overflowing in my heart by Your Spirit. That means I don't have to try to manufacture or work up love. It's in me! Your Spirit is empowering me to love You and others. I simply yield to Him today.

Glory by Degrees

We can all draw close to him with the veil removed from our faces. And with no veil we all become like mirrors who brightly reflect the glory of the Lord Jesus. We are being transfigured into his very image as we move from one brighter level of glory to another. And this glorious transfiguration comes from the Lord, who is the Spirit.

2 CORINTHIANS 3:18 TPT

Some people think the key to beating temptation is just somehow working up enough willpower: gritting your teeth, clenching your jaw, and declaring war on that recurring thought or stubborn habit. But willpower grounded in human strength eventually wears out. It turns out that willpower is an emotional muscle that, like all other muscles, grows weak and fails when its stores of energy are used up.

In the end, no amount of well-toned willpower is a match for sin. In reality, the more you try and say no with your own energy, the worse it becomes. The apostle Paul described this very struggle when he wrote, "For I do not do the good I want to do, but the evil I do not want to do—this I keep on doing" (Romans 7:19 NIV). Even the great apostle was intimately acquainted with the self-replicating cycle of defeat.

What is the answer? Paul lays it out beautifully in the very next chapter, Romans 8. Ending our futile dependence on personal willpower against temptation begins by recognizing that "there is now no condemnation for those in Christ Jesus" (Romans 8:1 NIV). Most believers wear condemnation like a veil in their relationship to God. Paul goes on to contrast living with our minds set on the flesh with a lifestyle of living with our minds set on the Spirit (see Romans 8:5–11).

The first produces only fatal, frustrating futility. The second results in life, peace, and victory. Now, this kind of life doesn't produce instantaneous perfection. What it produces is steady upward growth and progress. We move from one brighter level of glory to another. As Solomon put it, "The path of the righteous is like the morning sun, shining ever brighter till the full light of day" (Proverbs 4:18 NIV).

PRAYER OF DECLARATION

Abba Father, I'm glad that I don't have to trust in the strength of my own willpower to live in victory over temptation. Today, I take my eyes off myself and look at You, beholding Your glory with an unveiled face. I've removed the veil of shame and condemnation by receiving Jesus' righteousness. Simply living in Your presence is transforming me day by day.

I declare that I'm literally being transfigured from one degree of glory to the next! As I set my mind on Your Spirit and on spiritual things today, my path is growing brighter and brighter.

The Greatest Gift

He who did not spare his own Son, but gave him up for us all—
how will he not also, along with him, graciously give us all things?

ROMANS 8:32 NIV

Imagine for a moment that a rich and powerful prince falls wildly in love with a peasant girl and chooses her to be his bride. As a token of his love and devotion, he bestows upon her an engagement gift of extraordinary value and price. Now imagine that a few days later, she approaches him with a small but urgent need. Her cottage cupboard is out of bread. She asks if she might receive a loaf from his vast and ever-busy palace bakery. But her fiancé's response is "No. I love you, but you cannot have a loaf of bread."

If you were to hear of such a case, you would question either the prince's love or his sanity. And rightly so. After giving the object of his affection a gift of incalculable worth, it would make no sense to withhold from his beloved something as simple as a needed loaf of bread.

This is precisely the apostle Paul's point in Romans 8:32. To win our hearts and bring us into intimate relationship with Himself,

God has already poured out the most lavish and extravagant gift imaginable—His Son.

Yet, so often we approach our heavenly Father as if He is not wildly generous and unspeakably good. Or as if His resources are scarce. Our God is neither miserly nor poor. And He cares very much about even our smallest needs.

It is no accident that our sweet Savior's first public miracle was the simple provision of wine on a rural couple's wedding day. Running out of wine on your wedding day is not a life-and-death crisis. The parents would have survived the embarrassment before their friends and family, but it seems that to Jesus the mere prospect of their public humiliation was cause enough to draw forth wonder-working power.

He cares. God has given us His first and best. Everything else we need is small change.

PRAYER OF DECLARATION

Wonderful Father, forgive me for any time I have approached You as if You were anything less than extravagantly generous. Or if my heart has ever seemed to question Your goodness. Your gift of Jesus shouts of Your love and compassion toward me. What a gift! And when I see what He suffered on my behalf, I stand in awe of Your grace.

I declare that I will not insult Your extravagant love by coming to You as a beggar—or as if I need to find some way to overcome Your reluctance to supply my needs and bless. You are generous. Since You, dear Father, did not spare Your own Son, but gave Him up for me, how will You not also, along with Him, graciously meet my every need.

Abundant Mercy, Overflowing Grace

The faithful love of the Lord never ends! His mercies never cease.
Great is his faithfulness; his mercies begin afresh each morning.

Lamentations 3:22–23 nlt

The 19th-century preacher Thomas De Witt Talmage said, "The grace of God is abundant. It is for all lands, for all ages, for all conditions. It seems to undergird everything. Pardon for the worst sin, comfort for the sharpest suffering, brightest light for the thickest darkness."

It's true. God's grace is truly abundant. He has more of it than we can possibly ever utilize. And, we find His reservoirs of mercy topped off each new morning as well.

God's mercies and patience are inexhaustible. No matter how much we draw upon them throughout the day through our mistakes, frailties, and fleshly outbursts, each new morning we wake up to find God's mercy replenished to overflowing.

Even so, it is easy for us to slip into the same scarcity mentality shared by most people in the world. The fact is, scarcity may be a reality for people who have no covenant with the Creator of the universe, but that is not our reality.

> His divine power has granted to us **everything** pertaining to life and godliness (2 Peter 1:3 NASB).

> He has blessed us with **every** spiritual blessing in the heavenly places in Christ (Ephesians 1:3 NASB).

> He has equipped you in **every** good thing to do His will (Hebrews 13:21 NASB).

He is an *every* and *everything* Father. Scarcity is a lie of the enemy: an illusion, particularly where God's mercy and grace are concerned.

PRAYER OF DECLARATION

Gracious God, I thank You for the overwhelming abundance of Your grace. I purpose today to have an abundance mentality where all of Your goodness is concerned. I will access Your grace for every need and every circumstance. Great is Your faithfulness!

I declare that Your divine power has granted to me everything pertaining to life and godliness. You have blessed me with every spiritual blessing in the heavenly places in Christ. You are abundantly equipping me in every good thing to do Your will!

Seeing God

*The Lord passed in front of Moses, calling out, "Yahweh! The Lord!
The God of compassion and mercy! I am slow to anger and filled with unfailing
love and faithfulness. I lavish unfailing love to a thousand generations.
I forgive iniquity, rebellion, and sin."*

EXODUS 34:6—7 NLT

No human being in the Bible got closer to seeing God with his own eyes than Moses. The incident in our key passage took place as God was delivering the Ten Commandments to him. Customarily, an arriving king would be announced by a herald. The herald would go before the king, shout the monarch's name, and announce some of his attributes, such as the size of his armies and how many nations he had conquered.

God—alone with Moses on the cloud-shrouded heights of Sinai—has no worthy herald, so He announces Himself. He shouts His own name, "Yahweh! The Lord!" Now please notice what God chooses to cite as His defining characteristics:

Compassionate, merciful, slow to anger, with unfailing love, faithful, and forgiving.

This is how God introduces Himself. If the above is not our deeply rooted concept of the God we serve, we have some additional work to do in renewing our minds.

Did you know that you, too, have seen God?

You have seen Him much more clearly than Moses ever did if you have read the Gospels. Jesus was God revealed. He declared, "If you've seen Me, you've seen the Father" (see John 14:9). In other words, we don't have to wonder about God's nature, ways, or disposition—Jesus demonstrated it.

On every day of His earthly ministry Jesus loved, healed, received, welcomed, forgave, blessed, delivered, and comforted. This is a living, breathing picture of the God who adopted you and made you His own. You belong to a God of unspeakable kindness and compassion.

Yes, we have seen God. And He is wonderful.

PRAYER OF DECLARATION

God of compassion and mercy, how wonderful You are! Forgive me for ever doubting Your goodness or approaching You as if You were anything other than kind. I am mindful that Jesus vividly depicted Your nature and Your love.

I declare that You are compassionate, merciful, and slow to anger. Your love is unfailing. Your faithfulness is unwavering. You love to forgive and restore.

So, I come to You with a heart filled with gladness, gratitude, and expectancy. Let's talk. What would You like to say to me? What would You like to do through me?

Ask Big

"For it was I, the Lord your God, who rescued you from the land of Egypt. Open your mouth wide, and I will fill it with good things."

<small>PSALM 81:10 NLT</small>

Believers who have not renewed their minds to the reality of God's abundant grace come to Him with low expectations and small requests. There is a reason for this.

Their concept of God's character and disposition has been warped by religion. Their understanding of how wonderful our Father is, has been corrupted by a lying enemy. Satan used to stand before God and accuse people (see Job 1). Having been tossed out of heaven, he now stands before people and accuses God.

The terms and promises of the New Covenant literally sound too good to be true, so we're susceptible to the lie that they aren't true. This, in turn, produces a puny prayer life that doesn't ever seem to move very much of heaven to earth. Not surprisingly, coming to God half-convinced that He isn't good, and that you don't really qualify for help, answers, or favor is not a prescription for moving mountains.

Yet, God wants us to ask big. Indeed, He *needs* us to ask boldly and ambitiously because of the big things He wants to do on the earth through us. He has chosen to partner with us in extending His Kingdom and seeing His will done.

Jesus repeatedly gave us what is, in essence, a blank check: "Whatever you ask in My name, that will I do, so that the Father may be glorified in the Son. If you ask Me anything in My name, I will do it" (John 14:13–14 NASB).

Charles Spurgeon once pointed out that we are essentially insulting our great God by asking small. He wrote: "When we pray, we are standing in the palace on the glittering floor of the great King's own reception room. Shall we come there with stunted requests and narrow faith? Nay, it becomes not a King to be giving away pennies; He distributes broad portions of gold. Ask for great things, for you are before the throne of grace."

PRAYER OF DECLARATION

Father, I come before a great God on a great throne to ask great things. I will not insult Your grace by approaching You as if You are not utterly mighty, good, and generous. I come ready to partner with You in seeing Your will done on earth just as it is in heaven. By Your Spirit, inform and guide my asking!

I declare that the Lord my God rescued me from the domain of darkness and gave me a forever home in the kingdom of His dear Son. I will not insult my great King by asking small. I open my mouth wide, and You fill it with good things. I partner with my King in accomplishing great things in this world.

The Blood

He did not enter by means of the blood of goats and calves; but he entered
the Most Holy Place once for all by his own blood, thus obtaining eternal
redemption. … For Christ did not enter a sanctuary made with human hands
that was only a copy of the true one; he entered heaven itself,
now to appear for us in God's presence.

HEBREWS 9:12, 24 NIV

It is a wondrous, sobering thing to contemplate the reality that every new covenant promise made to God's people has been endorsed and sealed with Jesus' own blood.

We can be sure that these amazing promises that were sealed by His beloved Son's innocent blood are never absent from the Father's mind as we approach His throne. How could they be? It is by virtue of that blood that we can enter God's presence at all. As Charles Spurgeon once said, "Far be it from the everlasting God to pour scorn upon the blood of His dear Son."

As the writer of Hebrews reveals, "Therefore, brothers, we have confidence to enter the Most Holy Place by the blood of Jesus, by a new and living way that He has opened for us through the veil, that is to say, His flesh" (Hebrews 10:19–20 MEV).

To "plead the blood" can sound like an old-school religious phrase in our modern ears—a remnant of a bygone Pentecostal generation of tent revivals and camp meetings. This is a tragic loss because understanding the power and importance of Jesus' blood is a huge key to moving mountains in prayer. When we honor and acknowledge what Jesus' blood accomplished and sealed, our faith and confidence soars.

Spurgeon also taught:

> It is not possible that we can ask in vain with God when we plead the blood-sealed covenant. Heaven and Earth shall pass away, but the power of the blood of Jesus with God can never fail. It speaks when we are silent, and it prevails when we are defeated. Let us come boldly, for we hear the promise in our hearts.

When we consider and honor the blood that makes our access to God possible, demons tremble, the angels snap to attention, and God Himself leans forward.

IT IS BY VIRTUE OF JESUS'
BLOOD THAT WE CAN
ENTER GOD'S PRESENCE.

Prayer of Declaration

Father, I honor and gratefully acknowledge the indescribable importance of Jesus' blood. I come to You now—into the most holy place of Your presence—in His name and by way of His blood.

I declare that Jesus' blood has once-and-for-all-time washed away my sin-guilt. It has consecrated and sealed my covenant relationship with You. And it is by virtue of that blood that I now partner with You to carry out Your plans and purposes in my life.

Jesus' blood cannot fail. It speaks when I am silent. It prevails when I am outnumbered and surrounded. As I speak of the precious blood, demons tremble, angels snap to attention, and You, heavenly Father, lean forward.

Faithful and True

I saw heaven opened. And there was a white horse. He who sat on it is called Faithful and True, and in righteousness He judges and wages war.

REVELATION 19:11 MEV

The full, traditional title of the book of Revelation is "The Revelation of Jesus Christ." Setting aside all the difficulty and debate over the interpretation of this mysterious, final book of the Bible, we can be certain of one thing: in it we see the post-resurrection Jesus revealed in new and fuller dimensions.

One particularly striking portrait of the risen King is found in chapter 19: "His eyes are like a flame of fire, and on His head are many crowns. He has a name written, that no one knows but He Himself. He is clothed with a robe dipped in blood. His name is called The Word of God" (Revelation 19:12–13 MEV).

In Revelation 19, we have the reigning, ruling King Jesus leading His Kingdom armies forth as they make His enemies—sickness, oppression, injustice, lack, and all the other effects of the curse—a footstool for His feet. Yet in this fiercely vivid description, the first thing we learn of this awe-inspiring rider with many crowns is what He is called:

Faithful and True.

What a wonderful thing to keep in mind as we follow our Savior-King day by day, moment by moment. The object of our worship is *faithful*. The One into whose hands we have placed our lives is *true*.

He is the victorious, overcoming, conquering King, and we walk in His victory. We are not striving to overcome. We are in, and of, the One who has already overcome. And through His body—His people on earth—He is extending and expanding His rule: "of the increase of His government and peace there shall be no end" (see Isaiah 9:7).

PRAYER OF DECLARATION

Jesus, I rejoice in Your conquest of sin, death, Satan, and the curse. Because I am in You and You in me, I rest in Your victory. Most of all, I thank You that You are called "Faithful and True." I call You that, too. My trust is wholly in You today.

I declare that Your enemies are defeated and fleeing in my life. Sickness, oppression, injustice, lack, and all the other effects of the curse are becoming a footstool for Your feet. I follow You moment by moment today, for You are faithful and true.

Single-Minded Faith

If any of you lacks wisdom, let him ask of God, who gives to all liberally and without reproach, and it will be given to him. But let him ask in faith, with no doubting, for he who doubts is like a wave of the sea driven and tossed by the wind. For let not that man suppose that he will receive anything from the Lord, he is a double-minded man, unstable in all his ways.

JAMES 1:5–8 NKJV

We've explored the principle of heart confidence. The mystery of the power of a confident heart is embedded in the familiar words of 1 John 3:21–22 (NKJV): "If our heart does not condemn us, we have confidence toward God. And whatever we ask we receive from Him."

The equally valid inverse of that biblical statement would be this: "If our hearts *do* condemn us, we have *no* confidence before God, and *do not* receive from Him whatever we ask." This principle is echoed in James 1:5-8. The doubting, wavering, unconfident asker has a very hard time receiving from God.

The testimony of Scripture is that it is not the neediest or the most desperate who see miraculous answers to prayer. Nor is it the pious, self-disciplined, or "deserving" who find heaven's windows flying open when they pray.

No, it is those who approach and ask with the most confident hearts that see mountains move. And a confident heart comes by having a single-minded faith in the God's goodness and grace.

This is at once a great mystery and a liberating truth. It means that disobedience, or sin, does indeed damage our prayer effectiveness, but not for the reason we assume. We think God disqualifies us from getting answers from Him when we sin. The truth is, we stop getting answers because condemnation persuades us to disqualify ourselves.

How? Condemnation robs us of heart confidence—the factor that determines our capacity to receive in faith.

It's why the enemy of our souls spends almost all of his time and energy accusing and reminding us of all the ways in which we fall short. Satan (the accuser of the brethren) knows what many of us do not—that a confident, restful, believing heart is the key to keeping the windows of heaven open. It is the vital component needed for God to move His promises and provision into our lives and circumstances.

THOSE WHO APPROACH AND ASK
WITH THE MOST CONFIDENT HEARTS
SEE MOUNTAINS MOVE.

Prayer of Declaration

I come to You, Father, with a confident, expectant heart because I've been cleansed and made righteous through the blood of Jesus.

I declare that I am received and welcomed and favored by You because I am clothed with the flawless righteousness of Your Son. I now ask of You the things that I need. I have single-minded faith to receive all You have already willingly provided. I do not doubt. I do not waver in my assurance of Your goodness. My heart is confident before You.

Self-Disqualifying

So, friends, we can now—without hesitation—walk right up to God, into
"the Holy Place." Jesus has cleared the way by the blood of his sacrifice,
acting as our priest before God. The "curtain" into God's presence is his body.
So let's do it—full of belief, confident that we're presentable inside and out.

HEBREWS 10:19–22 MSG

As we have seen, confident expectancy before God is a major key to receiving from Him in prayer. However, for most believers, their approach to God's throne to ask for help or favor is encumbered by dozens of disqualifying thoughts:

I've sinned.

I haven't done enough.

I haven't followed through on that commitment.

I haven't had a quiet time in weeks.

I screamed at my kids.

Other people get answers because they are better Christians.

Amid this routine hailstorm of self-accusation and self-condemnation, many believers give up on even making a request of God. They tell themselves they need to get their act together and become a little more "deserving" first, then they'll petition God for help.

Those who do manage to make it to God's throne slink in sheepishly, laden with guilt and wrapped in a paralyzing sense of unworthiness. So, when their prayers prove to be ineffective, they're not at all surprised.

This pattern lies at the root of the exhortation in Proverbs 4:23 (NKJV) to "Keep your heart with all diligence, for out of it *spring* the issues [or forces] of life." It is vital to protect and maintain your heart confidence because it is the key to your capacity to receive from God.

When convicted of sin: confess it (see 1 John 1:9), count it as covered and paid for by the blood of Jesus, then mentally reassert your legal standing as righteous before God. It's helpful to continually renew your mind to the wonderful truth of Christ's finished work on the cross. Why?

Because through that work, you *qualify*. In Christ, you qualify for bold, confident access, connection, favor, blessing, and help in time of need.

CONFIDENT EXPECTANCY BEFORE GOD IS A

MAJOR KEY TO RECEIVING FROM HIM IN PRAYER.

Prayer of Declaration

Father, I rejoice and feel overwhelming gratitude that my access to You is not linked to my personal qualifications. I declare that Jesus has cleared the way for me by the blood of His sacrifice, acting as my Priest before You. My pathway into Your presence is His broken body and shed blood.

I come to You today in Jesus's perfect qualifications. I guard my heart against voices and messages that would move me back into thinking that my access to Your face and Your hand of blessing is in any way rooted in my own performance. I stand in Jesus' performance.

The First Exchange:
Our Sin for His Righteousness

God made him who had no sin to be sin for us,
so that in him we might become the righteousness of God.

2 CORINTHIANS 5:21 NIV

The cross is a place of exchange. We come to the cross carrying every cursed and awful thing that befell mankind in the fall. There we lay those things down, then walk away with our arms laden with extraordinary gifts. Yes, this seems too good to be true; but then the word *gospel* literally means "good news."

In fact, we make seven key exchanges at the foot of Jesus' cross. The more we understand, embrace, and proclaim these seven exchanges, the more grace-based—and therefore more powerful—our prayers become. The first of these seven exchanges is this:

We exchange our sinfulness for Jesus' righteousness.

Jesus became sin itself so that we might actually become the very righteousness of God. What an astonishing declaration. Yet it is absolutely true.

The prophet Isaiah was given a glimpse of the Messiah's future crucifixion and cried, "The Lord has laid on Him the iniquity of us all" (Isaiah 53:6 NKJV). The apostle John, who stood beside the Savior's mother on the day Jesus was crucified, described it this way: "This is real love—not that we loved God, but that he loved us and sent his Son as a sacrifice to take away our sins" (1 John 4:10 NLT).

Could anything other than real love offer a trade this lopsided? Jesus takes not only our individual acts of sin, but our *sinfulness*. In return, He assigns to us His righteousness. With it, we gain the amazing privilege of communion and connectedness to God that our forefather Adam once enjoyed but lost.

Jesus was made to be sin with our sinfulness that we might be made righteous with His righteousness. This is the first exchange available at the cross. It is a wondrous trade.

Prayer of Declaration

Oh, Father, what an amazing thing it is to know that Jesus took my sin and my sinfulness upon Himself and gave me His perfect, flawless righteousness. Help me, by Your grace, become continually more aware and conscious of this astonishing truth in the deepest recesses of my heart and mind.

I declare that I've exchanged my sinfulness for His righteousness. Jesus, thank You that You were made to be sin that I might be made righteous. In the process, I have regained the amazing privilege of communion and connectedness to You that my forefather Adam forfeited in the fall.

The Second Exchange:
Our Curse for His Blessing

Christ redeemed us from the curse of the Law, having become a curse for us—for it is written, "Cursed is everyone who hangs on a tree"—in order that in Christ Jesus the blessing of Abraham might come to the Gentiles, so that we would receive the promise of the Spirit through faith.

GALATIANS 3:13–14 NASB

From the very beginning, God's plan was for His people to live in blessing.

That extraordinary Garden into which He settled the very first people was a place of abundance, joy, peace, and beauty. It is no accident that the first words we hear God speaking over them were words of blessing: "God blessed them; and God said to them, 'Be fruitful'" (Genesis 1:28 NASB).

Of course, we know that when Adam and Eve rebelled, they let loose a horrific curse upon the earth in place of that blessing. Disease, lack, oppression, misery, strife, and pain suddenly reigned. Even the ground became cursed, refusing to yield provision gladly. For every one of the first couple's descendants, pain, hardship, and grief became the hard reality of life.

Yes, the first Adam released a curse upon the world. And yes, the earth still groans under the weight of that curse and will continue to do so until a new heaven and earth come along. But at the cross, the last Adam, Jesus, turned blessing loose in its place for those willing to humbly receive His offer.

The apostle Paul had this truth in mind when he told the Christians in Rome, "So just as sin ruled over all people and brought them to death, now God's wonderful grace rules instead, giving us right standing with God and resulting in eternal life through Jesus Christ our Lord" (Romans 5:21 NLT).

This is the message of our key verse as well. At the cross we get to exchange life under Adam's curse for Abraham's life of blessing. This is the second of the seven amazing exchanges we make when we accept God's gracious offer of salvation.

PRAYER OF DECLARATION

Father, what a privilege to exchange life under the curse of sin for a life of blessing under the rule of grace. Thank You that You have redeemed me from the curse of the Law, having become a curse for me, in order that in You the blessing of Abraham might come to me. I will not tolerate lingering remnants of the curse in my life or household under the false belief that it is Your will for me.

I declare that I have been to the cross and exchanged Adam's curse for Abraham's blessing.

The Third Exchange: Our Rejection for His Acceptance

He was despised and rejected by mankind, a man of suffering, and familiar with pain. Like one from whom people hide their faces he was despised, and we held him in low esteem.

<small>ISAIAH 53:3 NIV</small>

We all know that Jesus suffered for our sins, literally having our sins laid upon Him as He was crucified. Many of us are aware that Jesus also bore our sicknesses and infirmities, that we might know health and healing. But have you ever considered the fact that Jesus suffered the ultimate in *rejection* that you might experience the complete *acceptance* He knew as the Son of God.

He was despised and rejected by His people. He was betrayed and abandoned by His closest friends. But far beyond these cruel blows, as He became sin itself for us, He felt His own Father withdraw His comforting presence.

You will recall one of Jesus's cries from the cross was to quote Psalm 22:1 (NIV): "My God, my God, why have you forsaken me?" At the moment He made that statement, Jesus was experiencing the rejection *we* deserve. No human being has ever experienced such total rejection as Jesus experienced on the cross.

Jesus suffered your rejection so you might have His acceptance. You can purpose today to never again fall back into the trap of disqualifying yourself. You can learn to fight for your heart confidence: to feed it and strengthen it with God's Word and attack undermining, condemning thoughts with scriptural truth.

Fly to Him, child of God. Run as fast as your feet can carry you. Know that you are accepted, loved, and unspeakably welcome. Then, with grateful mindfulness of all He has done for you, pour out to Him your requests.

PRAYER OF DECLARATION

Father, I have been to the cross and exchanged my rejection for Jesus's acceptance. I stand in grateful wonder that He took on the rejection I deserved so that I could experience the acceptance He deserves. What a wonderful exchange.

I will maintain and protect the confidence of my heart before You. I will not fall back into the trap of disqualifying myself. I will not casually set aside such a costly and precious gift of Your acceptance. I run to the You freely and expectantly, knowing that I am as welcomed and accepted as Your Son.

The Fourth Exchange:
Our Sickness for His Health

But He was wounded for our transgressions, He was bruised for our iniquities;
the chastisement for our peace was upon Him, and by His stripes we are healed.

ISAIAH 53:5 NKJV

As we continue to examine the seven great exchanges we make at the cross of Jesus Christ, this brings us to Isaiah 53, which contains the prophet's prophetic vision of Jesus' suffering and death by crucifixion, roughly 800 years in advance of the event.

It is significant to note that Isaiah 53:5 is filled with the language of exchange and substitution. The Messiah received wounds for *our* transgressions. He was bruised for *our* iniquities. *Our* peace was purchased by His chastisement. His stripes—the marks of the brutal Roman scourging that preceded the crucifixion—brought about *our* healing.

We know that sickness and disease are not God's will for His people because there was no illness in the Garden. Pain and infirmity were not part of the lovely creation that God declared "good." Sickness was and is a result of the fall and its ensuing curse.

God introduced Himself to the Israelites as "The Lord who heals you" (see Exodus 15:26). Jesus attacked sickness and physical brokenness every time He encountered it. This is the same Jesus who declared that He only did what was pleasing to the Father (see John 8:29).

Through the centuries, there have always been Christians who do not believe that provision for physical healing was made in the atoning work of Jesus. Not surprisingly, these Christians see few healing miracles, which in turn only seems to confirm their assumption.

But among believers who understand that physical healing is an integral element in Jesus' atoning work, miraculous restorations are not unusual. Countless sick and suffering children of God have walked boldly into the court of heaven and received the provision Jesus purchased for them with His own body and blood.

At the cross, you can exchange your brokenness—spiritual, physical, and emotional—for Jesus' wholeness.

PRAYER OF DECLARATION

Jesus, thank You for everything You suffered and took upon Yourself in Your atoning death.

You were wounded for my transgressions, bruised for my iniquities; the chastisement for my peace was upon Your head, and by Your stripes I am healed. By Your grace, I will not let any of what You purchased go to waste or go unclaimed. You took my sickness and brokenness so I could have Your wholeness and health. I receive it.

The Fifth Exchange:
Our Shame for His Glory

...looking unto Jesus, the author and finisher of our faith, who for the joy that was set before Him endured the cross, despising the shame, and has sat down at the right hand of the throne of God.

HEBREWS 12:2 NKJV

In the Old Testament, we find two Hebrew words translated into our English word "shame." Though related, they describe two different sides of the human experience of shame.

The word *bosheth* describes the guilt and embarrassment we feel when our sin comes to light. It is *bosheth* that caused Adam and Eve to hide from the presence of God and sew fig-leaf garments. Every person with a functioning conscience has felt this shame.

The other Hebrew word for shame is *kalam*. This word is used to describe being hurt, rejected, disgraced, defiled, or humiliated—usually in public and particularly by someone close to you.

The first shame is that sense of uncleanness we feel when we sin, resulting in damage to ourselves or others. Its close companion is our English word *guilt*. The second shame is that humiliating sense of defilement and worthlessness we feel when we are used, abused, or wounded by others.

In other words, we feel the first shame when we hurt someone else, and the second when someone hurts us. The very history of the human race since the fall is little more than these two forms of shame simultaneously ravaging the souls of mankind generation after generation. Abusing and being abused. Defiling and being defiled. Hurt people hurting people.

Jesus experienced and carried both forms of shame with Him to the cross. When Jesus looked ahead to the cross, He didn't see pain, He saw unspeakable shame. Our shame—*bosheth* and *kalam*—being heaped upon Himself in almost infinite measure.

Oh, what shame Jesus bore on the day of His great sacrifice.

One of the great wonders of the cross is that Jesus did more than bear our sin. He bore the first great consequence of sin—our shame. No matter what we've done or what has been done to us, we are invited to come to the cross and leave our shame there.

Knowing this, why would we continue to carry a single particle of it?

No matter what we've done, we are invited to come to the cross and leave our shame there.

Prayer of Declaration

Jesus, I look to You, the author and finisher of my faith. For the joy that was set before You, You endured the cross, despising the shame. Now You are seated at the right hand of the throne of God. Thank You for pressing through—despising the shame—and enduring the cross for me.

I come to the cross and leave the guilt for my sin there. I leave the defilement and humiliation of every time I have been hurt or abused there, too. I will not insult Your grace or waste Your sacrifice by continuing to carry my shame. In exchange, I take up Your joy and innocence as my own.

The Sixth Exchange:
Our Poverty for His Abundance

For you know the grace of our Lord Jesus Christ,
that though He was rich,
yet for your sake He became poor,
so that you through His poverty might become rich.

2 Corinthians 8:9 NASB

The verse above explicitly states that Jesus became poor in order to effect yet another aspect of the great exchange at the cross. Many have debated the question: In what sense did Jesus *become* poor? It is clear that He did so in two senses.

First, He became radically poor the moment He stepped out of eternity and stepped into this fallen, broken, time-bound world. God the Son, the Word, laid aside the glory and splendor of heaven and moved into the frail, fragile body of an infant lying in a hay trough in a backwater Middle Eastern village.

Christ's birth stands as the most stunning drop in status and privilege imaginable. The apostle Paul clearly had this reality in mind when he wrote in Philippians 2:5–7 (NASB):

> Have this attitude in yourselves which was also in Christ Jesus, who, although He existed in the form of God, did not regard equality with God a thing to be grasped, but emptied Himself, taking the form of a bond-servant, and being made in the likeness of men. Being found in appearance as a man, He humbled Himself by becoming obedient to the point of death, even death on a cross.

Secondly, whatever possessions Jesus accumulated in His life were taken from Him on the eve of His death. At the trial before Pilate, He had nothing left but the robe on His back, a little physical strength, and His dignity. Soon even these would be stripped away.

The sinless son of God would soon hang naked and despised before a gawking world as Roman soldiers rolled dice for His garment. Never has a man been so utterly destitute as Jesus on that cross in those dark hours. He was poor in every way a person can be. No possessions, no comfort, no defenders, and no friends. But why?

So beggars like you and me could become children of the King.

We come to the cross to make a wonderful, absurd, unreasonable, too-good-to-be-true exchange. We bring our utter bankruptcy and leave it there, then walk away rich in love, hope, peace, power, and, yes, in abundant material provision for our every need.

Prayer of Declaration

Lord, what an extraordinary Savior You are. How unfathomable are the depths of Your grace!

I stand today in awestruck wonder and overwhelmed with gratitude for what You were willing to do for me and every other lost human soul. I declare that because of Your work on the cross, I am amply supplied, have all sufficiency in all things, and can therefore abound in every good work. You humbled Yourself and took on the form of a servant. The fact that You have freely given me all things frees me to do the same. I can serve and give and bless because I have been made rich in every way.

The Seventh Exchange: Our Death for His Life

Therefore, just as sin entered the world through one man, and death through sin, and in this way death came to all people, because all sinned … For if, by the trespass of the one man, death reigned through that one man, how much more will those who receive God's abundant provision of grace and of the gift of righteousness reign in life through the one man, Jesus Christ!

ROMANS 5:12, 17 NIV

There is a certain sad irony in the realization that we live in a culture seemingly obsessed with zombie movies and television series while the world is filled with people who are themselves a type of walking dead.

In His initial warning to Adam and Eve, God said, "You must not eat from the tree of the knowledge of good and evil, for when you eat from it you will certainly die" (Genesis 2:17 NIV). As we know, they ate anyway. Yet, they did not fall over physically dead the instant they disobeyed God's command. Nevertheless, they did die that day in a multitude of ways.

In that moment, physical death became a part of their future, and the future of their billions of offspring yet unborn. It seems strange, but in a very real sense, every one of us was born both dying and already dead.

This changes when it comes to the cross. And so, we come to our final exchange, the greatest exchange of all—our death for His life. Paul had this exchange in mind when he wrote to the Colossians: "You were dead because of your sins and because your sinful nature was not yet cut away. Then God made you alive with Christ, for he forgave all our sins" (Colossians 2:13 NLT).

It is a tragedy of unspeakable proportions when anyone dies without having made that exchange, a tragedy God sent Jesus to prevent. "For God so loved the world that He gave His only begotten Son that whoever believes in Him should not perish but have everlasting life" (John 3:16 NKJV). At the cross Jesus made it possible for us to exchange our death—in every form—for His life in every form.

"The thief comes only to steal and kill and destroy," Jesus told us. "I have come that they may have life, and have it to the full" (John 10:10 NIV). At the cross, you traded your life of walking death for one in which you are fully alive in every way.

AT THE CROSS JESUS MADE IT POSSIBLE FOR US TO EXCHANGE OUR DEATH FOR HIS LIFE IN EVERY FORM.

PRAYER OF DECLARATION

Father, how amazing it is to know that the power of death has been shattered in my life. Jesus has borne my death, and my spirit has been made alive by Your Holy Spirit. Yes, death once reigned in me through Adam, but I have been to the cross and exchanged my death for Your abundant provision of grace and the gift of righteousness.

I declare that abundant life in every aspect is mine—here, now, in this world. And physical death holds no sting for me, because You have gifted me with eternal life. Thank You for allowing Jesus to die my death, so I can live in Him and He in me. The same Spirit that raised Jesus from the dead is living, working, and flowing in me.

Hearing Is Following

"To him the doorkeeper opens, and the sheep hear his voice, and he calls his own sheep by name and leads them out. When he puts forth all his own, he goes ahead of them, and the sheep follow him because they know his voice. A stranger they simply will not follow."

JOHN 10:3–5 NASB

It is not unusual for a person who loses someone very dear to them to hang on to a final voicemail recording just to be able to hear their voice again. Our heart's reaction to hearing the familiar voice of someone who was so much a part of our daily life can be overwhelming. This is doubly true if it is a parent whose voice we might have been hearing since before birth.

The voice of your heavenly Father has much the same power to our born-again spirit. Even though our experience of hearing God's voice doesn't involve sound waves, when we hear it, something inside our hearts responds.

Jesus said, "My sheep hear My voice, and I know them, and they follow Me" (John 10:27 NASB).

Please notice that the Lord didn't say, "My sheep *ought to* follow Me." He didn't say, "My sheep *should strive* to hear My voice and, if they know what's good for them, they will *do their best to* follow Me."

The point is, Jesus' words are not a command to be obeyed. They are not an exhortation to be heeded. He simply made three statements of fact:

> My sheep hear My voice.
>
> I know them.
>
> They follow Me.

Notice the additional comforting promise in that same John 10 passage: "A stranger they simply will not follow." Hearing and following Jesus isn't a burden to try to bear; it is a promise to receive.

He knows you. You hear Him. You follow Him. Be at peace!

PRAYER OF DECLARATION

Oh, Good Shepherd, I thank You that my spirit hears Your voice and responds to it. The ears of my heart are attuned to Your voice. I receive guidance, instruction, direction, correction, encouragement, and comfort from You easily and clearly.

You are leading me beside still waters and restoring my soul. I lack nothing. You are supplying all my needs. I receive Your promise that a stranger's voice I will not follow. Where You lead, I'll follow today.

Stay in Grace

For if you are trying to make yourselves right with God by keeping the law, you have been cut off from Christ! You have fallen away from God's grace.

GALATIANS 5:4 NLT

For centuries, Christians were taught that Galatians 5:4 referred to people who somehow lost their salvation. To "fall from grace" entered the Christian vernacular as a phrase meaning to be rejected by God.

This is a terrible misreading of what the apostle Paul was communicating to the believers in Galatia. It comes from a lack of understanding of the nature of our new covenant of grace.

This becomes abundantly clear when we move back two chapters in Paul's letter and hear him scolding those believers who had embraced a teaching that in order to please God, certain aspects of the old covenant law—such as circumcision—had to be followed. Paul roared against this false teaching:

> Let me ask you this one question: Did you receive the Holy Spirit by obeying the law of Moses? Of course not! You received the Spirit because you believed the message you heard about Christ.

> How foolish can you be? After starting your new lives in the Spirit, why are you now trying to become perfect by your own human effort? (Galatians 3:2–3 NLT)

Jesus is our source. We stay plugged into Him by resting in His empowering grace. The moment we start striving to earn or merit God's approval by works, we are basically unplugging from our power source, or, in Paul's words, "cut off from Christ" having "fallen away from God's grace."

Paul reminded the Colossian Christians that we live the Christian life the same way we began it: by faith (see Colossians 2:6). Stay connected to your power source. Stay in grace.

PRAYER OF DECLARATION

Father, I come to You in no merit of my own. I come in Jesus' merit.

I stand in Your empowering grace through my connection to Your Son. I do not do good works to earn Your favor. Good works naturally flow from me because I already have Your favor. I guard my heart against messages from those who try to draw me away from grace by putting me back into the futile, fruitless treadmill of trying to earn Your love and acceptance.

I stay connected to Christ, my source. I began this journey by grace through faith; I will continue and finish it the same way.

Your Bubble of Favor

...to the praise of the glory of His grace,
which He freely bestowed on us in the Beloved.
EPHESIANS 1:6 NASB

God's glorious grace has been freely bestowed upon you in Jesus, His beloved Son.

The phrase "freely bestowed" is the Greek word *charitoo*. It has the same root as the words *charis* and *charisma*—which are usually translated "grace"—and it appears in only one other place in the entire New Testament. When the angelic messenger first appeared to Mary to let her know she was about to conceive the Messiah, he greeted her by calling her *charitoo* (see Luke 1:28)!

What does this unusual Greek word mean? *Charitoo* means "compassed, or surrounded, with favor." Paul declares that if you are in the Beloved, then you are constantly encircled by God's favor, just as Mary the mother of Jesus was when she was selected for the greatest honor ever extended to a human being.

Wherever you go, whatever circumstances you find yourself in, you go in a bubble of favor—predisposing people to listen to you, like you, receive you, and bless you. The psalmist David had the concept of *charitoo* in mind when he wrote:

> Surely, Lord, you bless the righteous; you surround them with your favor as with a shield (Psalm 5:12 NIV).

Some will read this promise and immediately disqualify themselves. They instantly think, *I'm not righteous.* Of course, for anyone in Christ, that simply isn't true. In Jesus, we have been made righteous with His righteousness (see 2 Corinthians 5:21). You don't get any more qualified for favor than that!

In Jesus Christ, you are *charitoo*—surrounded and shielded by an abundance of God's favor through the wonder of His grace. His favor goes in front of you before you even enter a room. It remains behind, working for you after you leave. You live in a bubble of God's favor.

IF YOU ARE IN THE BELOVED, THEN YOU ARE CONSTANTLY ENCIRCLED BY GOD'S FAVOR.

Prayer of Declaration

Father, Your grace is glorious and has been freely bestowed upon me in Your beloved Son. I thank You that I qualify to be surrounded by Your favor as with a shield because I have been made righteous with Jesus' righteousness.

I declare that Your favor is all around me. Wherever I go today, whatever circumstances I find myself in, I go in a bubble of favor. People are predisposed to listen to me, like me, receive me, and bless me. I will walk today in the quiet confidence that comes from the assurance that Your favor encircles me.

The Power to Bless

The Lord God has given Me [His Servant] the tongue of disciples
[as One who is taught], that I may know how to sustain the weary with a word.
He awakens Me morning by morning, He awakens My ear to listen as a
disciple [as One who is taught].

ISAIAH 50:4 AMP

Your words are more powerful than you know. This power flows from the spiritual reality that we are God's image-bearers in the earth—royal priests who carry Jesus' authority and grace—containers of His grace ready to spill out supernatural power to anyone in need.

This gives our words enormous weight in both the natural and spiritual worlds. Angels attend to our declarations. Things in the heavenlies move and change in response to our proclamations. And one of the most powerful uses of our words is the God-given power to bless.

The Greek word frequently translated "bless" in the New Testament is *eulogeo*. It means "to speak well of someone or something." In fact, it's the source for our common word "eulogy," which means "a speech in which a deceased person is praised and honored."

It is easy and tempting to turn our times of prayer into sessions in which we complain about others—often those closest to us. But there is far more power to effect positive change in words of blessing.

In writing to scattered believers everywhere, the apostle Peter said, "Summing up: Be agreeable, be sympathetic, be loving, be compassionate, be humble. ... No retaliation. No sharp-tongued sarcasm. Instead, bless—that's your job, to bless. You'll be a blessing and also get a blessing" (1 Peter 3:8–9 MSG).

It is indeed our privilege to come before God and speak words of blessing toward others, and to do the same as we go through our days. Blessing others is a gift from God. He gives us encouraging words of wisdom, and the supernatural ability to speak a word of refreshment to the weary. It is always by grace!

By the indwelling Spirit of God, you are abundantly equipped to speak blessing and create blessing everywhere you go.

ONE OF THE MOST POWERFUL
USES OF OUR WORDS IS THE
GOD-GIVEN POWER TO BLESS.

PRAYER OF DECLARATION

Father, thank You for making me a carrier of Your grace and a messenger of Your blessing. Thank You for showing me how powerful my words really are, and how they are a positive force for change all around me.

I declare that You have given me a well-taught tongue, and a supernatural ability to encourage the weary with refreshing words of grace.

I happily yield my mouth to Your Spirit today, Heavenly Father, to speak blessing and words of refreshment to the weary and discouraged.

The Adventure of Prayer

I was in the Spirit on the Lord's day,
and I heard behind me a loud voice like the sound of a trumpet.
REVELATION 1:10 NASB

In the natural realm, where we live in our natural, material bodies, we are bound by the laws of physics governing things like space, time, and gravity.

Space? We can only be in one place at one time. Time? The past is gone, we live in the present moment, and the future comes at us steadily and relentlessly one second at a time. Gravity? Well, hopefully you haven't had a hard lesson recently about its stubborn insistence on being fully in effect all the time.

The dimension of the spirit is very different. Jesus revealed, "God is spirit, and his worshipers must worship in the Spirit and in truth" (John 4:24 NIV). God is eternal. This means that the realm of the spirit lies outside the natural bounds of our space-and-time box.

Here is where our privilege of prayer gets very exciting. You live in a body, but the real *you* is spirit. As a born-again believer, because you are constantly united with the Holy Spirit of God, the

135

most important part of you lives constantly in connection with things that lie outside the constraints and confines of natural space and time.

Did you know that when you pray, in a sense you actually step over into the realm of the spirit with the Holy Spirit? In prayer, you are not bound by nature's stifling laws of time or space.

Distance means nothing. You can travel anywhere and impact events and influence the circumstances of others. And standing with God outside of time itself means you can pray into your own future and the futures of your loved ones. In fact, Jesus said one of the roles of the Spirit is to tell us what is to come (see John 16:13).

When we understand these truths, prayer is no religious duty or drudgery; it is an extraordinary adventure. An adventure upon which the Holy Spirit Himself wants to serve as our Guide (see Romans 8:26–27).

IN PRAYER, YOU ARE NOT BOUND BY NATURE'S STIFLING LAWS OF TIME OR SPACE.

Prayer of Declaration

Father, I stand in awe of the opportunity of prayer and the chance to partner with You in bringing heaven to earth, advancing Your plans and purposes in the world. By Your Holy Spirit, open my eyes to the unlimited, unconstrained opportunities to bring change, help, and miracles to the world and the people around me.

Although I live in a physical body, I am a spirit. So, in union with the Spirit of God, I travel the world and travel through time in prayer. Partnering with You in prayer, I step into eternity and change my circumstances, the lives of those around me, and the world. What a privilege. What an adventure!

Honeycomb Lying on the Ground

Now the Israelites were in distress that day, because Saul had bound the people under an oath, saying, "Cursed be anyone who eats food before evening comes, before I have avenged myself on my enemies!" So none of the troops tasted food ... But Jonathan had not heard that his father had bound the people with the oath, so he reached out the end of the staff that was in his hand and dipped it into the honeycomb. He raised his hand to his mouth, and his eyes brightened.

1 SAMUEL 14:24, 27 NIV

In a very real sense, the actions of Saul and Jonathan typify two ways to live the Christian life. Saul represents a fearful, insecure life of religious striving through works. Jonathan exemplifies the confident, abundant, victorious life rooted in covenantal grace.

God gave Jonathan and his armor-bearer a miraculous, overwhelming victory over a numerically superior enemy. The breakthrough was (literally) fueled by Jonathan's discovery of honeycomb just lying on the ground at the very moment he was famished and exhausted from fighting.

Saul and his troops came across the honeycomb, too, but they couldn't partake of this miraculous provision. Why? Because

Saul had placed himself and his people under a fast that was designed to earn them God's blessing and favor for victory. That victory remained only partial and incomplete because the people were too weak to pursue the enemy.

Here we have the perfect illustration of two ways of living. Saul's approach to life was characterized by fear (of both God and man), insecurity, and perceived scarcity. He hoped he could use works to *buy* God's help in advancing his own agenda. When God tried to bring him miraculous provision (honey), he missed it. *Religion* blinded him to God's provision.

In contrast, Jonathan's approach was characterized by security and confidence based on trust in God's covenant with him. He followed God's leading while assuming he had God's help and favor because he had adopted God's agenda as his own. When God brought him supernatural provision, he recognized it as the gift that it was and gladly received it.

Which approach to life in God will you choose: Saul's or Jonathan's? The fact is, God leaves honeycomb lying on the ground all around you because He is good. But only one of these approaches will free you to perceive it, receive it, and live in total victory.

GOD LEAVES HONEYCOMB LYING
ON THE GROUND ALL AROUND YOU
BECAUSE HE IS GOOD.

Prayer of Declaration

Father, I choose the way of Jonathan: the way of life rooted in a full understanding of Your covenantal grace.

I choose to abandon, once and for all, the life of fearful, insecure striving to earn Your favor and blessing. Because of Your faithfulness to our new and better covenant—one based on better promises—I have security and confidence. I follow Your leading, knowing I have Your help and favor. I've adopted Your agenda as my own. When You bring me supernatural provision, I perceive it and gladly receive it.

I embrace, today and for the rest of my life, the truth that in Jesus I am as loved, accepted, and approved by You as I can ever be. You have already supplied everything I need for total victory.

Praying Grace

So let us step boldly to the throne of grace,
where we can find mercy and grace to help when we need it most.
HEBREWS 4:16 VOICE

As a final exhortation, we must avoid the trap of turning prayer itself into a work. The fact is, the ever-present pull of our flesh is to turn everything good and spiritual into a work. The flesh likes to engage in works because it feeds our sense of pride. Most of us would rather *earn* rewards than *receive* gifts. Nevertheless, as we've seen, *grace* must be received as a gift.

After all, the Word of God describes the very habitation of our magnificent, reigning God as a throne of grace. Thus, the only way to come to Him is empty-handed but with a heart full of joyful gratitude for the privilege of coming before a King such as this. Good, compassionate, patient, and kind—this is the God who has chosen you to be His own.

Charles Spurgeon said it this way: "O, pray-er, why is your heart sad when you stand before the throne of grace? If it were a throne of *justice* you are approaching, you might have reason to despair. But you are favored to come before a King dressed in silken robes of love, so let your face shine with sacred delight."

God's throne is ever and always a place of mercy, grace, and help for you, His child.

THE ONLY WAY TO COME TO GOD IS EMPTY-HANDED BUT WITH A HEART FULL OF JOYFUL GRATITUDE FOR THE PRIVILEGE OF COMING BEFORE THE KING.

PRAYER OF DECLARATION

When I feel disqualified or unworthy,

I pray grace!

When I feel abandoned,

I pray grace!

When I am losing hope,

I pray grace!

When I am tempted to doubt that God is for me,

I pray grace!

When I feel discouraged,

I pray grace!

When I need a miracle,

I pray grace!

I qualify for all that Jesus suffered, died, and conquered death to purchase for me. When I feel unworthy, I don't avoid You, the Father who loves me; I run to You.

I come boldly and confidently—not because of any merit of my own—but solely because I have been clothed in Jesus' righteousness and merit. He has wholly and fully reconciled me to You. By the precious blood of Jesus, I have been cleansed from the shame and guilt of all my sin. Through His broken body, He has made available healing and wholeness for every part of my being.

I pray today and every day from this position of restful gratitude. It is not a throne of justice that I approach. It is ever and always a throne of grace.

About the Author

David A. Holland is a writer, speaker, teacher, husband, father, and grandfather carrying a call to help God's people better comprehend His goodness and grace.

He is the founding pastor-teacher of The Cup & Table Co., a growing network of house churches based in the Dallas-Fort Worth area wherein New Covenant truths are proclaimed, and the implications of Jesus' finished work are celebrated and lived out. His writing on faith, life, and culture is accessible at DavidAHolland.com.